# THE TOTAL
# TEACHER BOOK
# AND PLANNER

# Jossey-Bass Teacher

Jossey-Bass Teacher provides educators with practical knowledge and tools to create a positive and lifelong impact on student learning. We offer classroom-tested and research-based teaching resources for a variety of grade levels and subject areas. Whether you are an aspiring, new, or veteran teacher, we want to help you make every teaching day your best.

From ready-to-use classroom activities to the latest teaching framework, our value-packed books provide insightful, practical, and comprehensive materials on the topics that matter most to K–12 teachers. We hope to become your trusted source for the best ideas from the most experienced and respected experts in the field.

# THE TOTAL TEACHER BOOK AND PLANNER

### The All-in-One System that Gets You Organized, Empowered, and Inspired to Teach Your Best

## Lorraine T. Milark

**nea** NATIONAL EDUCATION ASSOCIATION nea.org
*Great Public Schools for Every Child*

**JOSSEY-BASS**
A Wiley Imprint
www.josseybass.com

Published by Jossey-Bass
A Wiley Imprint
989 Market Street, San Francisco, CA 94103-1741—www.josseybass.com

Jossey-Bass books and products are available through most bookstores. To contact Jossey-Bass directly call our Customer Care Department within the U.S. at 800-956-7739, outside the U.S. at 317-572-3986, or fax 317-572-4002.

Jossey-Bass also publishes its books in a variety of electronic formats. Some content that appears in print may not be available in electronic books.

*Library of Congress Cataloging-in-Publilcation data*
Milark, Lorraine T.
   The total teacher book and planner : the all-in-one system that gets you organized, empowered, and inspired to teach your best / Lorraine Milark.
      p.   cm.
   ISBN 978-0-470-43334-8 (paper/cd-rom)
   1. Teaching—Handbooks, manuals, etc.   2. Lesson planning—Handbooks, manuals, etc.   I. Title.
   LB1025.3.M544   2009
   371.102—dc22

                                                                                  2009019778

Printed in the United States of America

*PB Printing*              10  9  8  7  6  5  4  3  2  1

# CONTENTS

# PREFACE

Many years ago I heard Oprah ask the question, "What are we really here to do?" She said that, once we figure out what we are really here to do, real joy can't help but follow. I felt as if I had been hit on the head by a two-by-four once I began pondering that question. Allow me to explain. I consider myself an ordinary person. I teach, and I enjoy my students, I love my family and adore my friends. My journey until that point was wonderful. Like anyone, my life has had its peaks and valleys. While embracing life as an adult and earning a living, I was initially involved in the world of business. Later I earned a teaching degree and then a master's degree in counseling. I was passionate about teaching and chose to stay in the classroom while applying my counseling knowledge in private practice dealing with adolescent behaviors, grief management, and marriage counseling.

I embraced my classes every fall and continuously found them to be full of promise and hope. The school years flew by for all of us every year that I taught. I guess you could say I really enjoyed my job. Something else was continually happening over and over, and I did not recognize it until it was pointed out by others. Each and every class enthusiastically and consistently produced high test scores on the end-of-year state exams. Not a single year went by that my classes surprised not only themselves but me as well with their impressive test results. We'd share in the pride each and every time my classes elevated their grade level—or often the entire school—to recognizably higher-than-expected growth and accomplishments.

Although I was happy with my life, I felt that the time had come for a personal adventure. I had come to believe that it was not only prudent but also promising to change one's maps periodically. Getting out of our comfort zone saves us from working ourselves into a rut. I once had a professor who used to say that the only difference between a rut and a grave was the depth. So my husband Bill and I decided to make some significant changes—and change we did! All our children were grown, with Patty living in Colorado, Wendy in Beaufort, South Carolina, and Stacie just graduating from the United States Naval Academy in Annapolis, Maryland, ready to become a winged naval aviator.

It was time to spread our wings as well. Bill decided to buy a blue-water sailboat and we would follow the wind. Not having a lot of money, it was logical to travel at the expense of the wind. We could sail to places we had never been before, as well as to places we had already come to enjoy, but this time on our own sailboat. We eagerly began the process. Bill and I wanted to get off of life's treadmill and have the time and serenity to digest and perhaps better understand life's situations. We dreamed about clarifying and simplifying, and perhaps making sense of how we got to where we were in this game called "life."

We began downsizing, giving our children all that they wanted and getting rid of the stuff. Our children could not believe their parents were going to become nomadic, but they were totally supportive, and everything fell into place. At one time our house worked for us; now, we seemed to be working for it. We put it on the market and it sold immediately. After three huge yard sales and several trips to Goodwill, everything that did not fit on our thirty-seven-foot Tayana (an Asian-built, blue-water vessel that is very popular), named *Artemis*, was gone. I finished the school year and resigned my position. I closed the doors to my counseling practice, and Bill sold his trucking company. We simplified our life; over twenty-five years of accumulated stuff was now being enjoyed by many other people—theirs, no longer ours.

Our new adventure aboard *Artemis* began. Bill taught me how to tie lines and read charts, and we learned how to plot our course. We met countless fascinating people everywhere we traveled. We also came to discover a whole new culture:

people from every walk of life who, like ourselves, decided to leave their comfort zones in search of their own personal adventures aboard their own sailing vessels, catamarans, and trawlers. We were educated daily in a wide variety of new subjects. A life of making incredibly interesting new friends and sharing life's lessons with people who were from so many unusual walks of life was sincerely a great deal of fun!

In the midst of incredible tropical islands, sailing adventures, wonderful people, and beautiful places (not to mention water so clear and spectacular in color it often appeared too enchanting to be real), I began to feel terribly unproductive. I know this sounds ridiculous. I thought so as well. But I felt the need to keep teaching. This was so bizarre; initially I just shook my head and asked myself, "What in the world is this all about?" I did not think I really missed the classroom. How could I? I was enjoying a lifestyle we both devoured, yet something was amiss for me; I didn't feel that way all the time at first, but I was certainly aware of a void. I decided the void would go away if I became involved. With so many needs surrounding me, I decided to work with students who were preparing for exams, to tutor children, and, of course, to do seminars and counsel many frustrated parents.

I continued to try to stay busy in education any way I could. It was fun doing seminars because lots of interesting people asked for workshops on a number of topics. I spoke on anything I was trained to share: teaching strategies for parents, addictive behaviors, codependency issues, relationship concerns, and grief. Our only son Billy had died in a traffic accident when he was only sixteen. I remember the compelling sadness and changing family dynamics that took place as we all dealt with our grief in very individual ways. We, as a family, held each other so closely, but that is not to say we did not all experience different levels of extreme hurt and healing. That tragic time in my life was one that later made a powerful difference.

It was so enjoyable visiting all the many different schools on each of the islands we visited and observing different ways that things were accomplished. Meeting the different children and staff members was enlightening. Some children attended school in crisply ironed uniforms and listened attentively as I told them stories about students in America. Other youngsters were taught barefoot in a single building that accommodated every child on the island of Rum Cay in the Bahamas. All the learning took place in this one building that had no phones, no audio video equipment, and almost no books, making me realize how very much the teachers had to work with in the United States.

All the same, I missed teaching regularly in a classroom. During this time both Bill and I were able to read a great deal, thinking about things we never really had the time to think about before. This led us to do some serious soul-searching. Together we adopted a lifestyle that advocated going with the flow, no longer swimming upstream whenever we could help it. We practiced acceptance and nonjudgmental behavior. Together, we agreed that allowing life's situations to steer our ship was far easier than fighting the tide. Recurrently, we learned that we could not control the wind but that we certainly could and would adjust our sails (an old Yiddish proverb has been the mainstay of how we live still). A friend of mine made me a patch depicting what Gayle LaSalle tells us: "We cannot change the direction of the wind, but we can adjust our sails."

Based on this knowledge, we practiced listening to that little voice deep inside of us and acknowledging what we were being told—from within! We were taking a time out in order to tune in to what we were really all about and what we were really here to do. So we compromised. We decided that we could sail back to a stateside working boatyard. Bill would really enjoy taking care of some necessary tasks on *Artemis.* She was certainly good to us, and it was now time to give her some long overdue TLC. We would stay in touch with our cruising friends by way of single sideband radio and e-mail. We committed to waiting until after hurricane season was over and then we would rendezvous with our group. We would once again travel south and wait for an appropriate weather window to make the annual trek across the Gulf Stream, headed for another extensive stay down island. *Artemis* would be recommissioned, and we would be on our way. What a plan!

One day in August, friends who lived in North Carolina, near the working marina where we hauled *Artemis*, invited us out to lunch. As we drove into town, I noticed the board of education building and asked whether we could please stop for just a moment so I could run in and ask about a substitute position. I did just that and left my name, number, and e-mail. By the time we returned to the marina from our trip to town, there was a message for me at the desk. A substitute position was available in fifth grade beginning immediately. The students were returning to begin the new school year in just two days, and the position had not yet been filled. Not knowing how long the position would be for, I gladly accepted. I quickly put together about six outfits that I could get by with and not look too much like a boat person.

The following morning I found myself in a small coastal school, which almost every staff or faculty member had attended as a child. Many faculty members were related to the students. My six outfits were perfect. The atmosphere was very casual. The guidance counselor, as well as the science teacher and coach, wore shorts every day. The principal was delighted to have the position filled on such short notice—a dream come true for everyone involved. The fifth-grade teacher I was substituting for had a very ill family member (her youngest child) and needed a leave of absence for an unspecified amount of time. She did not want to lose her position, and I certainly did not want a full-time position, making me very nonthreatening to her in this time of difficulty. It was a win/win situation all the way around. This was meant to happen. I was really sure of it now. I remembered reading the powerful words of Solomon Ibn Gabirol, while enjoying my cruising lifestyle down island:

> In seeking knowledge, the first step is silence, the second listening, the third remembering, the fourth practicing, and the fifth teaching others.

Teaching and living in Beaufort, South Carolina, for almost three decades and then going sailing all over creation, I now found myself in a position in Beaufort, North Carolina, spelled the same, pronounced differently—so strangely serendipitous!

Let's once again reflect on that perpetual question: "What am I really here to do?" That question and its answer have been presenting themselves to me time and time again for many years. I just never realized what was transpiring. Over and over I was oblivious to what was taking place in my classroom every single time I taught. I now know that I must share what I learned: *The children have had the answers to our national problem all along.* Before diving into this, I'd like to include you in another situation that emphasizes the certainty I feel about this.

When our son Billy died on that awful day March 16, when he was only sixteen, he kissed me goodbye at about 7:30 that morning, told me he loved me, and left for school. I never was hugged by him again. Sadly that afternoon at 3:16 he was killed in a traffic accident.

I am sure you can understand when I say that our entire family's life went topsy-turvy, with stomach–wrenching pain and hurt. We were so incredibly sad. Billy was fun. Billy was vibrant, Billy was so sweet and so very young, having so much still left to accomplish. My birthday is July 15, Billy's birthday was July 14, and we always did something special together, just he and I to acknowledge that we had a special bond. We always made a point of making it a "new" something. Once we played tennis for the first time. On another occasion we took a walk on a new part of the beach. Once we went to a new store and shopped, just the two of us. His sixteenth birthday was the last time we did that. Billy left a similar, yet unique void within each of us. We cried, we shared, we grew, we wondered, we hurt, and we all began asking, "Just what is life all about?" I personally began reading, sharing, inquiring, and trying to put our family back together again. At times, I'd rearrange furniture only to find one of Billy's socks or unpack the Christmas decorations only to hold tightly his favorite ornament; every part of my life was less because of his absence.

Life somehow manages to go on. From time to time, difficulties continue to present themselves. We were certainly not exempt from life's continuous tests. Each time I'd be down or upset, Patty and Stacie, who were both still living at home, would wink and say something like, "Yes sireee, that stinks, but, hey Mom, at least there are no empty seats at the dinner table!" Wow, how resilient children are, how wonderfully accepting, and how much they can teach us if only we respect them enough to listen to understand rather than, in most cases, listen to correct or condemn. I have come to know that each year I taught children, they in fact taught me far more than I taught them. Therein lies the answer to our problems. We must know how to ask the right questions then simply *listen*.

Our problems in education *can* be repaired. The students have the answers, and they have been shouting them at us for far too many years, but we have been turning a deaf ear. We need to listen to what they are saying and see those red flags they are waving. A very special class, the class that brought their school to first in the state for most improved, was comfortable enough with the boat person who became their fifth-grade teacher, to share and to spell out the situations that we need to correct. Yes, we the educators are not above being corrected! We really need to leave our egos at the door and accept that it's time for a shift in education.

With all those experiences on my life-living resume, by the time I became that boat person teacher, I was ready and willing to *listen.* I was receptive. I was at a time and place in my life, comfortable enough with life itself to digest what the students (the real teachers) were saying. I implemented what was necessary. They proved (as all the subsequent classes since then also proved) that new thinking works. What they shared was valid! The beginning of the Total Teacher was really that class. They had the answers, and I listened. This experience validated that the students are ready, that they want to learn, but that they need teachers with a new mind-set in order to make the connection: teachers who are ready, willing, and able to listen to the students.

What happened after I gave in to the overwhelming desire to return to the classroom really got my attention, as well as the attention of many others. The students spoke, as they had for many years, but this time someone listened, someone understood, someone validated their concerns and comments, and their thoughts and ideas. I really heard with a piercing clarity not only what they were saying, but what their parents were saying as well. I listened not to reply, but to understand. Now, for all the children everywhere, I will share what they and their parents are saying and how you too can listen to understand. If you do, you will let wonderful things begin to happen to you as well as to the students in your care.

*Lorraine T. Milark*
April 2009

*A very special dedication*

the *total* teacher® is for all teachers and their students

however none of this would be possible without the love and
support of my husband and my best friend

Bill

Thank you for making my life beyond complete!

# THE TOTAL
# TEACHER BOOK
# AND PLANNER

# INTRODUCTION

☐  Are your students well behaved?

☐ Are they devouring your subject matter and the standards they have to master?

☐ Are you graduating them to the next grade with solid As and Bs?

☐ Are they at Proficient and Advanced levels, rather than Below Basic or Basic?

☐ Are you going home with little or nothing to do, so that you can take off that professional hat and put on your personal hat?

☐ Is there enough time for you to do some things for yourself that provide the balance you need for sanity?

Probably not many teachers can answer yes to all or even a few of these questions, but as a Total Teacher, you will be able to. After writing my first book I was asked to make time for more and more personalized classes, conferences, and trainings. Each workshop became better than the previous one, because the Total Teacher philosophy of empowering the students and asking the right questions continues to bring more and better information front and center, positively and productively enhancing the lives of all who attend.

This book will bring *you* that information, with a new way of thinking about old things. You'll be given all the information that will enable you to turn things around and make your classroom function exactly as you know it can. It will also provide you with the balance that you know you deserve in your personal and professional life, in and out of school. As the Total Teacher you will have more time, more balance, more control and insight into your students, into yourself, and into your profession.

We teachers know that teaching is what we were born to do. Teaching is the one thing that most of us have truly enjoyed doing ever since we can remember. But soon after we became teachers, we became part of "the system," where we—far too quickly—found ourselves silently screaming, "Just leave me alone and let me teach!" It often seems that all we were inspired to be, to do, to say, or to create slowly gets taken away from us. We do the things we have to do in order to keep our jobs, even though we know that so many of those things are just not working. We go through the motions day after day, week after week until we are tired, frustrated, and upset because we are being forced to dance someone else's dance—a dance that is full of outdated steps, with a beat neither we nor our students enjoy let alone relate to; a dance consisting of meetings, standards, disruptions, assessments (oh, those assessments!), announcements, commitments, observations, deadlines. The list goes on and on. Anyone can take a look at the state of education today and quickly figure out that something is terribly wrong.

Take a breath, smile, and know that this is about to change. You owe it to yourself to take a new look at some old thoughts. You are *not* a failure or even slightly ineffective. You are torn! You are truly torn as you try to jump through hoop after hoop, and day after day the results often get more and more disastrous: students complaining, parents unhappy, classroom management a mess, and, worst of all, no time to get it all turned around. You know that there has to be a better way, an easier way to get the job done. This book will share the tricks of the trade, real and relevant solutions, and a new way to get the job done and leave the insanity behind. What you have is an insight into a new way of thinking about many things, a total new outlook.

# Total Teacher-*isms*

My system is based on a number of principles, or what I call Total Teacher-*isms*. Let's look at them one by one.

### Change the Way You Look at Things, and the Things You Look at Change

For example, look at two simple words that demonstrate this point really well:

- Reactive.

- Creative.

The words both have the same letters; they're just arranged differently. But that difference is key. When you *C* things differently, you can become *creative*, more positive, more proactive, and more creatively productive. When you choose not to *C* things differently and reactive, you tend to become negative and defensive.

We often work very hard yet feel as though we get *nowhere*, but if we think about that differently and appreciate the present moment, we can think we are *now here*. Again the same letters are the same, we just see them differently!

I guarantee that my new information will empower you with new thoughts, allowing you to enjoy new ways of engaging yourself and your students and changing any negative perceptions to productive and positive ones. You will find yourself at the head of your game, proudly embracing the best profession in the world: teaching!

Like many of us, you've probably been handed many books that have been circulated for years, attempting to tell us how to be better teachers, how to do the job right. These books are filled with wonderful ideas that look great on paper, but I would just once like to see these people come into my classroom and make it work in the long term. That is why I still spend so much of my time actually in classrooms, not just for brief visits, but taking over the entire day and field-testing the newest and most effective strategies.

So often people seeking help get pounded with information that is not relevant to *their* issues or not compatible with what is already in place, and that sort of information just makes matters worse. At the start of each conference or Total Teacher workshop, I ask those in attendance to identify their monsters. No, that does not mean the students who don't behave or who can't do the work they are given. The monsters are *ours!* The monsters are *our* issues, *our* concerns, and *our* problems that we carry with us into *our* classrooms. The monsters are the things that we wish we could remove from our professional and sometimes personal lives because they make getting the job done impossible. Isn't it time we stopped and identified the issues that are real to us? Once identified, the issues *can* be rectified.

Yet, for educators, there is often no time even to think, let alone identify things that truly need to be rectified. We all know that when the bell rings, we have about two minutes to get the class to the media center or cafeteria or get them on task. Often we are not informed of the fire drill, the practice lockdown, or the tornado drill that takes place just when everyone finally settles down. We begin our days with about 25 people wanting our undivided attention, and if we aren't ready, willing, and able, things simply fall apart.

Once the obstacles—the monsters—get identified, and you change the way you look at them, they begin to look different and you are able to rectify them one by one. It feels great! No matter where in the country I go, the monsters are the same. Make your own list of monsters before you look at the ones I will share.

My monsters are:

_____

_____

_____

_____

_____

_____

_____

Here are some of the monsters that appear over and over as I conduct workshops all over the country:

- Student apathy

- Not enough time

- New programs, being told what to do at the last minute

- Lack of respect and discipline

- Too many rules

- Teaching on grade level

- Lack of communication

- Negativity (usually really prevalent in the teacher's lounge)

- Poor work ethics

- Parents who are not supportive

- Complicated state standards

- Noisy and unruly students

- Lack of administrative support

- Too much paperwork

There are very real and easy to implement solutions to these concerns, or monsters. Once you learn how to change the way you look at things, the things you look at change, for you, for your students, and for everyone else involved.

People do not take kindly to being *made* to do things. A simple shift in thinking will allow you create the *want* to get things done with a new sense of pride and accomplishment! This new thinking shifts the responsibility and the wanting from you to the students. It's amazing. Once you change *your* dance, other people change their reactions to your new actions. The responsibility of learning truly becomes the wanted responsibility of the student, which is where it needs to be. As you learn how to create the *want* to learn or to do something, rather than trying to *make* others learn or to do things, you begin getting the results you want. Isn't that what it's all about? Isn't what you want the joy of being able to create successful outcomes, your way?

## Students Take on the Personalities of Their Teachers

Just think about how very enlightening this Total Teacher-*ism* becomes. We all know it to be true but either don't want to admit it or choose to avoid a sometimes painful truth. When teachers are overwhelmed, unhappy, or frustrated, so are their students. Let's process this from a different perspective. Do you feel that you are simply not interested in another "new" program? Do you feel as though you have heard them all? Do you wonder when you no longer will be told what page to be on or exactly how to present an objective on any given day at any given time?

This is exactly the kind of thing the students are feeling and saying as well. "I don't understand." "It doesn't make any sense to do it this way!" They've heard it all before time and time again—and so have we. It didn't make sense the first time because it wasn't relevant or valid, and it doesn't make sense now.

When teachers are excited, engaged, enthused, and empowered, so are their students.

Ghandi, another incredible teacher, tells us: "We must be the change we want to see." That is a powerful statement and a fundamental truth. We must change *our* dance in order for our students to do things differently. We can't make anyone do anything, but if we change our dance, our steps, and our methods, the noise turns into beautiful music. You lead, the students follow, and the dance continues. If this is not where you and your students currently are, if you are not currently dancing this wonderful dance in unison, you must stop and change your music. Stop doing what you are doing, or you will just keep getting what you are getting.

From being in synch with your students, you will learn new and better ways to foster change. We want to stop self-defeating behaviors and encourage a rhythm of joy and growth. We want our students to blossom, to do the work, and to absorb and retain the massive amount of available information. We need to remember that no student–teacher relationship is ever successful unless the student's perception of him- or herself is in positive alignment with the teacher's perception of the student. If we let students know that we truly believe in them, that we know that they can accomplish so much, and that we will help them set great but attainable goals, they will surpass all expectations. When we are capable of conveying this message of trust to them, when we *demonstrate the trust* and not simply tell them about it—demonstrate that we believe in them—it happens: The dance begins to rock. Then students start to say, "OK, I've got it!" The *aha* light goes on, and in no time they are off like a shot.

## To Teach is Not to Learn

I want you to pretend that you are one of about 30 people entering my class-room. You will be in my room for the next 40 to 55 minutes. Once everyone is seated and I have welcomed them into the room, I begin doing squats—yes, physically moving up and down with my hands straight out in front of me. I explain that I am an outstanding squatting teacher. I can squat slowly or quickly. I squat because I know that being healthy is vital. I teach squat-ting because the act of squatting for 45 to 55 minutes each day will tighten your glutes, take away any flab in your arms, tighten your tummy muscles, and do wonderful things for your metabolism and your hearts. I tell each of you in my class that I am a nationally board-certified squatting teacher, that I really know my subject matter inside and out, and that I can engage in the process with expertise. I share that I have many certificates and degrees to prove how good I am at teaching my standards of squatting. The next thing I say is, "OK, class. Everyone now stand. We will all now begin squatting and will continue to do so for the remainder of the class."

How does that make you feel? Are you eagerly jumping to your feet and, with an abundance of enthusiasm, beginning your squats? I don't think so. Here is the point: I am trying to *make* you squat. Replace the word "squat" and the act of squatting with the word "read" and the act of reading, or with the word "math" and the act of figuring out word problems, or with "social studies" and the memorization of state capitals. Students of all ages will react pretty much the same way you did: They no more *want* to read, to work out math problems, or memorize capitals than you want to squat. Just because a teacher is up there teaching doesn't mean the students are learning.

## We Must Give People What They Want in Order for Them to Accept What They Need

It is more apparent than ever that our classrooms and our teaching methods are terribly outdated, and our students know it. They are our customers, and we are not giving them what they want. What causes these happy, enthusiastic, energetic young people, who love school initially, to change their attitudes? What makes them eagerly look forward to all that happens in those early years, then have a change of heart? What causes them to not want any part of learning or attending this place we call school? This change certainly cannot be viewed as a natural evolution. The business of public education is losing its customers; they are going elsewhere. One reason is that students are afraid of failure.

This brings us to another Total Teacher-*ism*.

## Effort is Directly Linked to the Expectation of Success

Unfortunately, far too many students have little or no expectation of success (in squatting or reading or dividing or multiplying). Year after year, many of them try to jump through all the hoops and to do what is expected, and their effort is rarely enough, nor is it interesting, nor is it what they *want* to do. In many cases it is not even something they *can* do because they don't understand what is being said. We need to identify that far too many students are turned off and feel defeated because we have a communications gap long before we experience an achievement gap. They do not apply themselves at times when it is so important to do so. Why should they? Oh, there was a time when they tried and tried, but they reached a point where they are convinced of ultimate failure: "Why bother? It's overwhelming; I don't know what they want or even what they are talking about." Eventually they no longer try, instead looking for something else to do: make spit balls, throw paper, talk to a friend, and so on.

We perpetuate feelings of inadequacy in so many students because we have not come to truly believe that we must encourage failure in order to promote success. The child who gets reprimanded for "not getting it" over and over ceases to try. When we encourage failure and simply explain that there are stages to learning and improving, learning becomes something students want to do.

I like to compare this point to that little tool that we all use at one time or another at a gas station: the air pump. When the tire on our car is low, we remove the valve cover, put the tool on the stem, and *inflate* the tire. The interesting thing is that same tool will also *deflate* the tire, if applied at a little different angle. So it is with children. Through our reactions to their attempts at learning, we can inflate or deflate them. When they have little or no expectation of success and are not encouraged to fail in order to succeed, failure becomes unbearable, and they quit.

## We Win Because of What We Know, and We Lose Because of What We Don't Know

Teachers really do not have enough time in the day to teach everything that needs to be taught. This is why we need to inspire our students so that they *want* to learn. Our job is said to be creating lifelong learners. If we are doing all the talking and teaching and that is the only way that our students get the information they need, what takes place all weekend, or in the evenings, or all summer when the teacher is not there? If we are doing all the talking and the teaching (and we now know that to teach is *not to* learn), how is the mastery of information taking place? It's not! Obviously there is fundamental flaw in the process! We don't see the things we need to see, but it's not your fault. Let's look at something that is a lot of fun, the FED EX arrow:

How many of you know that there is an arrow between the *E* and *X*? Probably not many of you, even though you've seen countless Fed Ex trucks, planes and vans. At one of my many workshops, a young lady raised her hand and asked me, "Ms. Lorraine, do you see the spoon?" Someone else then said, "What about the egg or the upside-down bowl?" The point I was making was that we are often so busy that we can't even digest what is happening right in front of us. This response from the participants also proved to me that, collectively, our students know so much more than we do. And if we engage our students, they begin raising the bar much higher for themselves than we are ever able to do for them. (By the way, the spoon symbol is in the *e* and so is the upside-down bowl. The egg is in the *d*.)

So here's one more Total Teacher-*ism*.

## Excuses are Made by Those Who Need Them!

We complain that our students are responsible for:

- Low test scores

- Apathy

- Inappropriate behavior

- Dropping out of school

- Lack of responsibility

- Lack of organization

- Poor manners

- Absenteeism.

Education as we know it today has all of these and many more concerns. However, the truth is that I never had to deal with these concerns. Instead, my classes and I experienced:

☐ High benchmark test scores

☐ Outstanding grades

☐ Extremely motivated students

☐ Ecstatic parents and administrators

☐ Attendance improvements from previous years

☐ Responsible and organized young people

☐ Very impressive state standardized test scores.

Let me add that now thousands of Total Teachers nationwide can say the same, and they have impressive testimonials of their own!

Obstacles are not reasons to fail. When I first began teaching, I spent one year teaching first grade. Teaching little children how to learn to read for the first time is a very rewarding challenge. My scores were some of the highest the school had ever experienced, and I was presented with the faculty award of excellence that year. I was then asked to move to sixth grade math and see whether we could improve those students' outcomes. This position entailed teaching adolescents in a departmentalized middle school. I had 150 students that year. The students moved around a great deal because many of their parents were involved in very transient types of work. That year I taught math six periods each day. Our final math scores were improved by over 70 percent that year. The following year the scores continued to rise. I was asked to be the grade-level chairperson and gladly accepted. These impressive outcomes happened year after year. As I moved on, they occurred in schools where the student population was over 95 percent minority, in military schools with incredibly high student turnover, and in schools for children of migrant farmers.

The real awakening was when, once again, this happened after I had not been teaching for several years and I was totally unprepared. I had no accumulation of all that helpful "stuff," such as notes, content familiarity, and teaching aids. Also, this was a temporary setting, in a new state I had never worked in before, with a different curriculum and a different testing process, and I did not even have an inspiring wardrobe or a car to get me back and forth to work in a good frame of mind! In addition, there were limited teacher editions (none for core subjects as the teacher took them with her, and the school did not have multiple copies). Yet the results were again positive: super-high scores, tremendously happy parents, and not only great grades, but also very motivated students.

## The Total Teacher Plan

Eventually, I realized why my classes were so successful. It's about a system, a method, a plan, that works. It's a well orchestrated plan that is easy for anyone to follow, a plan that was created by listening to my customers (my students) and by taking a cue from the world of business. The plan encompasses the 180-day school year with 30 Fridays to do the job, then being able to review.

When people are genuinely engaged, empowered, and enthused in productive and rewarding accomplishments, whether personal or professional, they respond with growth and gratitude. When students, parents, or principals are included in the way you conduct your business of education and in your place of business, your classroom, everyone responds. The stress-free productive environment is conducive to success.

As the Total Teacher, you will understand that you are in the business of education. You have a product to transfer (to sell). That product is knowledge (the standards). If you know how to sell your product correctly, the customers (the students) buy it, want it, and learn all they can about it. If you do not know how to transfer the product correctly, they are not interested. They leave; they check out.

The Total Teacher plan can be used at every grade level and in a self-contained classroom where every subject is taught by one teacher or in a departmentalized setting where every teacher teaches one subject. It works in settings where relocation is frequent and disruptive, and it works in rural, poor areas as well as in wealthy metropolitan schools and charter schools. And when applied to an entire district, the academic momentum and positive morale are increased dramatically.

Once you start using the Total Teacher plan, you will enjoy the best career there is: teaching our young people! Raising test scores in a courteous, rule-free learning environment is not only possible, it is probable and practical. How rewarding it is to watch children leap out of their seats with joy because they aced a test. How satisfying it is to hear parents express their gratitude with statements like, "My son now loves school. You don't have any idea what that means to me." . . . "Last year my child wanted to quit.

Now he is thinking and talking about college." . . . "My daughter never tried this hard before. Now she is applying herself and she wants to learn everything that you are teaching." These types of outcomes are what teaching is all about. As in any profession, however, one needs the right tool to do the job correctly. Every action begins with a thought, and we must therefore change the way we think about education.

Throughout this book I want you to make notes in the margins, anywhere it moves you, and to highlight or underline the things that seem to jump out at you. Energy is a very real force and should not be dismissed. Countless books have been written about changing our reality, and they all have a fundamental theme: Our thinking is where we must begin.

This book will introduce you to all that makes the Total Teacher plan incredibly productive: new thinking, new timelines, and a new rationale for performing a job in a better fashion than ever before in order to meet the needs of your customers.

We've already learned that knowledge alone does not change behavior and that people's attitudes change when their experiences change. As you begin learning about the Total Teacher plan, you will want to put some of its components in place immediately, and they will inevitably change, not only because of your experience in the classroom but also the experiences of your students. Your new strategies will transform the energy of your audience from a position of being forced to a new and engaging empowerment for all as they *want* to learn. Every student deserves the Total Teacher.

So let's begin dancing a whole new dance, with a newfound energy and excitement! Remember, as Oliver Wendell Holmes tells us: "Man's mind, once stretched by a new idea, never regains its original dimension." The Total Teacher will introduce you to new thinking and to new strategies, and it will stretch your mind as you come to enjoy this new dimension. Let's begin our journey!

# The Total Teacher Philosophy

*There Has to Be a Better Way to Do This!*

*The man who can make hard things easy is the educator.*

RALPH WALDO EMERSON

*In teaching children we must seek insensibly to unite knowledge with the carrying out of that knowledge into practice.*

IMMANUEL KANT

*You go into an audience and ask people to go back over their childhood and pick out teachers that did the most for them. I think you will find in every case that they will say such and such a teacher waked them up, or such and such a teacher first inspired them. They will put it in different ways. They may have forgotten whether she was a good disciplinarian or not. The mechanical teachers will note the ones they will speak of;*

*it will be the teachers that rouse them, that got hold of them. That means the teacher that found the mental trait that was uppermost in the pupil and that succeeded in giving it intellectual nutriment in such a way to make it grow. The child did not know this trait. The other teachers did not find it out; but through some natural instinct, this particular teacher defined what was going on in that mind and succeeded in making connections, this is the great object of education.*

JOHN DEWEY

There is a way for *all* teachers to be like the teachers described in these quotes. It's about a plan and an insight into new thinking that enable teachers to become Total Teachers. Success does not happen by using a conglomeration of other people's ideas and methods. Instead a Total Teacher learns how to convey the sincerity of his or her own philosophy. The approach is genuine, becomes contagious, and creates leaders at every level! In a Total Teacher classroom there is a plan and a place with a very different look and feel that creates a brand new potential. Little tricks of the trade create a new kind of classroom where untapped potential explodes with a positive and productive attitude.

## A New Way of Thinking About Your Students

My background is in three diverse disciplines that are vital to making the Total Teacher successful: business, counseling, and teaching. I believe that a teacher must know about and use fundamental thinking in all three of these areas.

## Teachers as Businesspeople

As *businesspeople*, teachers are in the business of selling education, in a real sense, to students, their consumers. When teachers shift their own thinking to that of an intelligent, creative employer, they generate the want to learn in students who feel like productive employees almost immediately. Employers, of course, do not do all the work; they know how to create an enthusiasm that engages their workers with a work ethic to get the job done. So why is it that teachers feel that they have to do all the work of teaching? In today's standards-based classrooms, the teacher realistically does not have enough time to teach it all. However, if the teacher knows how to create the want to learn, students will be inspired to complete far more work on their own while learning and mastering their state standards. It's what good employers do. It's part of a total business plan!

## Teachers as Counselors

Teachers are also *counselors* because they must know how to listen to understand, not just listen to reply. Children's emerging self-esteem is very much affected by us, their teachers. Think about the child who hates math because a teacher had poor teaching methods, which perhaps embarrassed the child. There is also the child who deems herself a failure at writing because all those things she wrote and thought were great were never quite good enough for her teacher. I am not advocating that everyone get a prize or be patronized. The point is rather that it's not what you say but how you say it that can either encourage or discourage a child.

### The Power of Drawings

I've learned what countless psychologists have known for years: Children love to be expressive through their drawings. For instance, one first-grade student asked me whether I could identify a drawing when I was visiting his classroom. He told me the artist was Picasso and couldn't I tell that he was sometimes the angry artist! Children truly have so much to say, and what they have to say comes across as they play and create.

Alfred Adler tells us:

Play is a child's work and this is not a trivial pursuit.

Playing and drawing are natural processes of expression for children that can provide so much assistance to the teacher. Think about the times you say to your class, "Ladies and gentlemen, I have to go talk to the principal for a moment. While I'm gone, please take out a blank piece of paper and quietly draw." They are all thrilled and do it. Then we often collect those drawings and throw them away, never even realizing they are full of pertinent information. Children want to invite you into their worlds; as a matter of fact, they desperately want you there. They need to be understood and to bond with their teachers, and this is one way they do it naturally.

Children can't wait to draw, so let them! You will be amazed at how much information comes across in this, their favorite way of communicating their innermost feelings, fears, needs, and expressions! Make time to do this; it is so easy.

Here are a couple of examples of how I approach the process.

Let's take a break, ladies and gentlemen [*Addressing students as adults is far more empowering than saying "boys and girls" at any grade level!*] Hmmm, let me see, I would very much like you to draw me a picture. Yes, I'd like you to have you draw me a picture of a person walking in the rain.

They can't wait to get started. I ask them please to realize that this is a serious assignment. Soft music in the background helps them concentrate and adds to classroom peace. Have them do the drawings with just a black pencil on a plain unlined piece of paper. As they draw, they will be unaware that you will learn so much about them through their simple renderings. They will give you a clear insight into their dispositions under stress. Is the child at this time in his life coping or not coping with his current situation?

Here is your crash course in interpreting the drawings.

- If the drawing is complete with the person in the rain protected, with perhaps an umbrella, some protective clothing, and maybe rubber boots, the child is dealing relatively well with stress at this time in her life.

- The type of rain and how much there is can also give you an insight into just how vulnerable the child currently feels.

- If the drawing shows the child standing in the rain with no protection, no umbrella, or no rain gear, then the child is relatively unsure about new situations.

- Often the child who feels vulnerable will have obvious tension in his strokes.

- Other readable indicators include a dark cloud directly overhead or no visible signs of hope or brightness, such as a sun in the corner or a flower.

Of course, these drawings change as the child's perception of things change.

When the drawings are complete, ask students to sign and date their creations. You can turn this into a writing assignment at any grade level by asking them to write a short story or poem about their drawing thereby giving them a chance to better explain their artwork if they want to. It validates their creativity and can give you further helpful information. In addition, the child gets the first of many messages that says you care, you think she is worthy of recognition, you enjoy spending your time looking at the drawings and stories.

Another example is having students draw a picture of their families. Begin by sharing with them that you know very little about their families and that you think a drawing might give you some insight. Knowing what to look for in these drawings is almost self-explanatory.

- The sizes of the other family members in the drawing are in direct proportion to how important they are to the student. The figure they label as themselves may be the same size as the others, indicating that they perceive themselves on equal footing.

- Often an only child who is very spoiled and used to getting his own way will be much larger than mom or dad. This child knows that he is in control. This child will probably have a real adjustment problem being in a room with twenty-five "equals." How helpful to you to identify that early on. Your understanding of why this child is having a problem will allow you to deal with the situation much more effectively.

- If in the drawing the student is close to mom and dad and a bit smaller in size, the child is probably comfortable in a traditional home setting.

- Often, if there is a new baby in the home or some turmoil that makes the child feel alienated, she will unconsciously place herself away from everything else that is part of his family.

At least once a month, I take about twenty minutes out of any given day and have the class draw me a picture. To them it's just a fun break, but to me it's a wealth of current and interesting perceptions! New books and information dealing with art therapy and current issues are readily available. I would also recommend taking a class or two in art therapy, because the training can help you uncover some serious issues in your students that can then be addressed. For example, sharp aggressive strokes, perhaps even the beginning of a picture that is so suddenly and rapidly erased that it tears the paper, *could be* a waving red flag and should be taken up with a counselor.

### The Environment for Growth and Change

It is very important to set up an environment with procedures in place that allow students to grow and change. Total Teachers lend themselves to the art of being flexible and proactive rather than rigid and reactive. When we listen to understand rather than listening to reply, our questions get different answers. Total Teachers respect their students enough to ask them how they plan on getting to where they want to go. To encourage reachable short-term success, for example, you might ask questions like, "Where do you see your-self by the end of the week?"

The powerful words of Solomon Ibn Gabirol have empowered me with new thinking while enjoying my cruising lifestyle down island.

> In seeking knowledge, the first step is silence, the second listening, the third remembering, the fourth practicing, and the fifth teaching others.

Here is how that will work through you: When the student is ready the teacher shall appear!

- The student will first be *silent.*

- The student will then *want* to *listen* (rather than be *made* to listen!).

- The student will then *remember* all of your positive input and prac-tices (and *want* to reciprocate).

- The student will then begin *practicing* what you've modeled and advocated. (The teacher institutes the change. Remember, as Gandhi tells us, "We have to be the change we want to see.")

- The student will share and model new behaviors that will *teach and inspire* others in the class to *want* to follow!

As teachers, we need to realize that command and control methods no longer work. We truly need to make a shift, and Noam Chomsky says it beautifully.

> We should not be speaking to but with. That is the second nature of any good teacher.

### *An Anger Management Strategy*

Before leaving these counseling strategies and moving on, I feel that addressing a simple strategy to help with anger management is helpful. Total Teachers probably deal with a lot less anger and stress than their colleagues; however, I feel that knowing how to use ongoing counseling techniques can be enormously helpful in creating really good classroom management. Today anger is a huge problem that is not properly dealt with because so many districts do not know how to address anger and rage in a proactive way, rather than in a reactive fashion. Behind most anger is fear, and students are fearful of many things, one of which is failing. We must realize that students truly begin their educational process wanting to learn but that they often become angry when they try to experience success and continually fall short. This is equally true for students who feel that no one is listening to them.

Allow me to share a neat way to deal with anger spontaneously in the classroom.

Ask everyone to get on their feet. Grab a big box of crayons, a radio, and a long piece of bulletin board paper, maybe fifteen feet long. Walk all the students over to the cafeteria if it is not in use, or perhaps to the gym, out in the hall, or even (and preferably if it's nice) outdoors. Drop the paper on the ground, and have all the students sit or kneel around the large rectangle of paper. Spread the crayons out along the length of the paper and say something like this:

> Here are the rules. Ladies and gentlemen, when I begin playing the music [*pick something classical and soothing, and, of course, tell them the name of the piece and the composer*], you will begin drawing something, anything at all. When the music stops, you will stop as well and shift one seat over to your right. That will put you in front of another drawing that has already been started by a classmate. When the music begins again, please begin to enhance the drawing in front of you, the drawing that has already been started. You can add to it, modify it creatively, or do whatever you want to it, but simply make more of the drawing that has already been started by someone else. When the music stops, we will once again, stop, shift, and begin drawing on the next drawing. We will continue doing this until you end up back where you began.

Once they are back at their own creation, lead the class in a discussion of this question: "How does seeing your drawing now make you feel?" Some will be angry, some disappointed, others amused, and still others confused. Feelings, emotions, perspectives—which are all different, all unique, and all important—are all now being experienced, shared, and understood. So much is mastered in this very enjoyable and life-altering process. Then explain the point of the exercise: "Life does not always turn out the way we plan, but it is our choice as to how we will adapt and react to what takes place."

Each time I engage a class in this demonstration of self-reflection, the students want to take the mural back to the room and display it. Why? Because students are brilliant, because they want to learn, and because they want to remember what they learn. They also are now introduced to a higher level of communicating their feelings at any given moment.

### Gauging the Students' Emotional Level

I also hand out a "How Do You Feel Today" sheet I have had for years, and then have another conversation. (See Figure 1.1.)

If your school counselor is receptive, workshops can be conducted to give teachers the skills needed to be more effective counselors in the classroom. This lightens the load for the counselor, and teachers learn how to use phrases and techniques that are not taught in most of the training that teachers receive. For example, if you repeat the exact words a child uses back to her, you demonstrate that you listened and really heard and understood what she was trying to convey and her thoughts are quickly validated.

## Teachers as Teachers

Putting yourself on the students' emotionally expressive level is very important! From time to time, stop and share that you too mess up royally. I typically share some of my many human blunders, like the time I sprayed my hair with spray starch, a direct result of my not thinking when I am doing things too quickly. This teaches them so many lessons: We are all humans who make mistakes, but we can laugh at ourselves, learn from our mistakes, and increase our educational vocabulary by understanding that we can delight in and identify with many emotions! We also share that it is never appropriate to laugh at someone else. Doing so certainly does not make you look educated or compassionate. Mini-chats about life, while bringing yourself to their level, lets them know that

Figure 1.1 How Do You Feel Today sheet.

**How do you feel today?**

|  |  |  |  |  |  |  |
|---|---|---|---|---|---|---|
| Angry | Anxious | Apathetic | Ashamed | Blissful | Confident | Confused |
| Creative | Depressed | Determined | Disappointed | Disbelieving | Enraged | Enthusiastic |
| Envious | Exasperated | Exhausted | Frightened | Frustrated | Grateful | Grieving |
| Helpless | Hopeful | Hurt | Indifferent | Insecure | Inspired | Jealous |
| Joyful | Lonely | Meditative | Miserable | Negative | Obstinate | Optimistic |
| Pained | Passive | Puzzled | Regretful | Relieved | Resentful | Sad |
| Satisfied | Shocked | Sick | Sympathetic | Threatened | Triumphant | Withdrawn |

you are honored to be on their team. Tell them that, and let them know that it was not so long ago that you were sitting in a classroom just like this, "Let's see that was just about one hundred years ago." They laugh, and we continue.

## Bridging the Communication Gap

Many of us grew up in a different era when it was appropriate for children to be seen and not heard, and often we carry that mentality into the classroom.

But we must remember that in a learning environment questions are crucial. Each and every lesson must end with the opportunity for questions and comments that can be accomplished in a multitude of ways. One example of valid feedback is an exercise that can be carried out orally as you dismiss your class or in writing on simple index cards handed to you as they depart, for you to review at your leisure. I call this the 1-2-3 method:

- One thing I learned about . . .

- Two things I'd like to know more about . . .

- Three things I want to go over again . . .

It can be that or any such combination. This feedback provides you with information and students with validation. They immediately realize that their thoughts matter in this classroom. Referencing any combination of their feedback from the following day empowers and engages everyone.

Children are entitled to be understood. When children do not have the skills to accurately express themselves, we have to step up to the plate. They can't pick up the phone and make an appointment with a counselor when they feel lonely or hurt emotionally. They often do not know how to discuss shyness or anger or anxiety. I am not suggesting that we can fix all the areas that are askew; I am suggesting that we can make our 180 days each and every year far more positive, productive, and powerful for all involved. We need to recognize that the teacher can be the child's closest confidant and counselor. We as teachers need and deserve the tools that allow us to understand and to do all we can to bridge that communications gap. Once the communications gap is bridged, we see the achievement gap disappear.

Let me give you something else to think about. If we, the teachers, are doing all the teaching, what happens when we leave? What happens when we stop teaching, such as during the summer or when we are just not there? Learning often stops when teaching stops. However, if we know how to create the want in students to become lifelong learners, the mission is accomplished and the learning continues forever.

### Appreciating the Individuality of Students

All people are different. For each of us, there are some things we just cannot tolerate and other things that we enjoy immensely. Understanding these differences in your students is very helpful. For example, one student wants to read and reread every word of the book he is enjoying, often going back and reading it again and again, perhaps not even caring whether the book ever gets completely read. Another student may want to read the jacket, the topic sentences, skim over the rest of the paragraphs, and then take the test! Which one is correct? Neither is "right"; they are just different. Once we realize this as educators, accept the differences, and learn how to use them to our advantage, our jobs get incredibly easier. I have attended countless workshops on teaching styles but was rarely informed of ways to blend all those needs with my goals and with the standards and keep them student centered! I often heard of superficial Band-Aids that realistically accomplished very little.

Understanding the personality of a student and of yourself is vital. The Meyers Briggs, a wonderful personality assessment that can be found online, is a helpful tool that can help you discover much about yourself and your students. For example, once you come to realize that a student is not unfriendly but merely an introvert or shy, you can pair that student up with an extrovert, or an outgoing student, and they can learn from each other's strengths.

Once we appreciate each and every one of the students and their differences in a new way, we can send them many new, positive messages.

This creates an outpouring of brilliant, previously untapped potential. Using terms such as, "No kidding, I didn't know that" to a student makes her feel a foot taller. Asking a student to repeat a statement makes him feel that his opinions are valued: "Wow! That was so powerfully stated, would you mind repeating that so everyone can digest what you just said?"

You begin accepting every student as unique and special. It becomes the instructor's obligation to help students rid themselves of a failure identity and instead adopt a success identity and assume the responsibility for their own behavior. We are not here to change them or restrict them, but to educate them and, most of all, to transfer responsibility for their fullest potential from others to themselves. We must facilitate, inspire, motivate, and encourage them to see, feel, and experience all that an education can and will bring them. We have the opportunity to bring out the positive or the negative. It's all about modeling and knowing where you are going.

### Sending the Right Messages

The messages we send are so important. So are the messages we don't send! Being aware of how messages are received is just as vital as articulating how they are conveyed. Every year I cover the largest bulletin board in my room with two messages that we all sign after we feel that we understand them and are capable of implementing them on pretty much a day-to-day basis, or at least trying to implement them.

The messages are:

- EFFECTIVE COMMUNICATION IS ALWAYS, KIND, GENTLE, AND RESPECTFUL!

- THE PROBLEM IS NEVER THE PROBLEM, IT IS THE ATTITUDE ABOUT THE PROBLEM

When students (or adults) are unkind, disrespectful, or less than gentle when communicating, the message is rarely effective because the other person shuts down, ceasing effective communication. Students can be encouraged to "self-check" their means of communication to see whether it meets all three criteria: kindness, gentleness, and respect.

The second statement can be explained by holding up a glass filled halfway with colored water and asking the proverbial question: Is this glass half full or half empty? The question is not how much water is in the glass; it is how we look at things.

### The Value of Making Errors

Another important strategy of Total Teachers is to put a new spin on errors. Total Teachers know how to share mistakes in positive ways. This enables students to learn from one another and creates an atmosphere that shifts those dreaded blunders into positive territory, something that has to take place in a true learning environment. The classroom then becomes a safe place to work, learn, and experiment. If our students already did everything perfectly, they would not need to attend school. When this new freedom is conveyed and felt by our students, they raise the bar immediately. They accept the idea that it is vital to make mistakes because it is those errors, those storms at sea, and those bumps in the road that we learn from, that give us character, and that help us make better choices. Mistakes become viewed as gifts that bring deeper understanding to why and how things do or do not happen. They create great teachable moments that allow us to ask, "What was my lesson in this?" This shift also helps create the desire in students to continue learning forever. That does not happen if students are penalized for, or embarrassed by, making mistakes, as demonstrated by today's incredibly high dropout statistics. The creation of this new classroom environment begins with the teacher—the Total Teacher!

In my own classroom I always had a huge eraser that said, "For Big Mistakes," and a sign that described a fundamental belief:

It is perfect all right to make mistakes; that is why there are erasers on pencils. Educated people learn from those mistakes and try not to make them again.

I have interviewed countless new teachers, and almost every one of them tells me that college did not adequately prepare them for the classroom. It can be extremely frustrating for a teacher to begin a new year and know very little about the children in the class. Often important occurrences are not shared, and there is little background information on this person who is going to be part of your group for the next 180 days. Of course, you could read their "cumes" (cumulative folders, which I'll explain shortly), and they would be somewhat helpful, but what is that child like today, right now? There is no reason why a classroom teacher should not have the availability of new information, current information—a snapshot into who this student is right now. Being able to access this information is just as important as knowing how to check for understanding. We must be in touch with the total student. Does a child have vital information that really needs to be shared with you, but can't because he doesn't have the skills to transfer this information? We certainly do not want to stand up in front of the class and put a child on the spot by saying, "Just tell me all about yourself," yet that is often how it is done.

Teachers have access to cumulative folders, but they are among the best kept secrets as far as the students are concerned. Students often get all the way to high school and are not aware that information about them has been accumulated in this folder. This very important folder keeps track, year by year, of everything that takes place concerning that student. It is complete with pictures, personal and professional information, both positive and negative, and it follows the student all the way from kindergarten to graduation. However, teachers often need more information, which can be generated by having the students fill out job applications and resumes instead of doing that same autobiography over and over, year after year. When you start the year off this way, instead of students thinking about (and often dreading) coming to school for the next 180 days, they think about going to work. This small mental shift encourages them to feel and behave like young adults at work rather than as little children at school. You may be surprised to learn that most students never make basic connections that adults take for granted, such as realizing that they come to school in order to prepare for the world of work. You can easily create or purchase a job application that encourages students to expound on all that they can do or have accomplished. Students enjoy this empowering grown-up process that allows them to introduce and validate themselves.

## A New Type of Student Notebook

*I* also strongly advocate this dual-purpose Total Teacher strategy: students taking notes in homemade books and later using the books as review tools. Students enjoy note taking, and these homemade notebooks make the review process fun. Give them help when they are taking notes. Here are a few suggestions:

- Use initials, like "LRD" for "little red dog" instead of writing all the words out.

- Even at the high school level there is something intrinsically motivational and personally validating about students' making their own books and using them for their own notes rather than using store-bought binders.

- Put important information on the board in an abbreviated fashion so that students get into the habit of writing down just the important words and statements.

- If there is a handout to the lesson, students may add notes to the handout and include the handout in their notebook.

- Young students learn the art of note taking very quickly by using highlighters. As you and they read together, point out things such as topic sentences, important adjectives, proper nouns, and other criteria that later become fundamental to note taking. They will enjoy adding highlights to their notes.

- Middle school students are usually very into their own artwork, and this becomes a true motivator at an age when often they are not the least bit interested in taking notes or remembering facts.

Be sure to have students wait until all the notes are completed before they illustrate the cover. This is extremely motivating, creating a new academic inspiration. Then allow them to pick whatever subject they want to draw on the cover. Anticipation coupled with choice goes a long way to validating the note-taking process. Another motivating technique is allowing them to draw small pictures on the page numbers to help them remember what notes were on what page.

These notebooks become great review tools. You will now learn how each quarter we pass out only one-third of the state standards that are to be mastered. We begin with a clean slate each marking period. This becomes an opportunity to raise the bar and not be labeled, stuck, or penalized for days past but to move forward with visible improvements. This method of beginning anew every marking period allows students to rethink what they did the previous quarter and to make appropriate modifications that are especially enjoyable in their own personalized note-taking books. When these booklets are all given back to the students at the beginning of the last quarter for the review process, they eagerly compare how much better their most recent note-taking books look compared to their first, immediately recognizing their own growth and maturity. This is a new and wonderful feeling and experience for many students. You've just empowered your students with intrinsic motivation, setting the tone for wanting to become lifelong learners.

## A New Way of Teaching the Standards

*A*s described in the previous paragraph, a Total Teacher strategy involves providing the students with a copy of what they are expected to learn. Thousands of students rarely see, understand, or get to keep their own copy of the standards, the "stuff" they are responsible for mastering! Our students are held accountable for and will be tested on material that they often never see. In the world of business, employees receive a tangible copy of what they will be responsible for, so giving students a list of standards, which are *their* responsibilities, once again validates that these students will be treated like competent employees, as young responsible adults. This also complements the effects of having them create a job application and resume.

Starting out with the entire list of standards would overwhelm even the highest achievers. Instead, I give them a list of the standards broken down into thirds, with each third passed out at the beginning of a quarter or marking period. The goal is to have the first third mastered by the end of the first quarter, the second third mastered by the end of the next quarter, and the final third mastered by the third quarter, leaving a full quarter to review all the standards prior to testing. Your team spends the final quarter furiously reviewing and having fun while others are still playing catch-up!

You will find that many of the standards have been taught many times before in previous grade levels, with some mastered but many not. Once you give your students a copy of the standards in thirds, they can break into groups with highlighters and identify which standards they already know, which ones they've seen many times over, and which ones are totally new to them. Do this as a class lesson initially. The students will have the standards (first third) in front of them, and you will begin the discussion.

The first thing you need to do with them is to simplify the very difficult language of the state standards, allowing them to better understand what they are looking at. Let them know that you are all in this together. As you discuss the standards, you will probably have a good laugh at how the standards, as written, often make something simple sound incredibly complicated. Your students will see that there is a communication gap and come to realize that failure to master the standards in the past may not have been their fault! This conversation will set them on a new journey, a long overdue journey of self esteem and a new desire for learning. This is even more effectively accomplished when the entire district is involved. When many teachers put their heads together, it is easy to divide the standards sensibly and to blend them with districtwide benchmark testing. But you can do it just as easily for yourself, your way.

When I teach standards with practical student-centered application, transference, and conversation, the process is very rewarding for them and enjoyable for me. I have created simple processes that will allow students to self-check and learn quickly. This process brings out the potential of all the students and also creates a very easy grading system. Students take each standard and ask themselves the TTTA questions. Are they are able to:

- **T**each the standard.

- **T**ransfer the standard to their world.

- **T**ake a test on the standard.

- **A**pply the standard to the adult world.

When teaching the standards, I check for understanding at least two times each hour so that the students are aware of whether they know a standard. It's easy to give a four-question quiz, plot it on a Curve, and see who really heard what you were teaching. The aha light quickly goes on, and students become aware of a simple truth: Some people answered all four questions correctly, some only answered one question correctly, and so on. This gives them immediate feedback concerning whether they really know the material and how they compare to the rest of the class. The test is fair because there were only four questions, and they were all about things you taught during the previous 20 minutes!

Another great motivating activity is to have your students earn sticky notes or index cards as proof of mastery of each standard. Once they really know a standard, meaning they can TTTA it: teach it, transfer it, take a test on it, and apply it to the adult world. They then write that standard on a sticky note or index card and stick it on the month that they mastered that standard. This creates transparent accountability! If you chose to test them or simply ask them to apply a standard to their world—or the adult world that they are preparing for—and they can't do it, their signed standard mastering card comes down, but it rarely does. They are very proud that they really know the standard before they post it. This lends itself to the most motivating competition ever, raises your students' test scores, and makes you look outstanding.

## New Ways of Keeping Track of Time

We often overlook the fact that students are not time sensitive. Once we realize this, it becomes easier to provide the tools students need to manage their time and get everything done.

## The Syllabus

First, students, even in elementary school, should receive a syllabus. The syllabus is an outline of your game plan that lets everyone in the class know where you are going. Having a grade-appropriate syllabus at every grade level is vital. The syllabus should also be posted for all to see at all times.

## The Calendar

I was in the business world long before entering the world of education, and quite frankly when I became a teacher I was shocked at what I found. My very first week in this new profession made it painfully obvious that the business of education was in serious trouble. I just could not visualize myself functioning in the constraints of the traditional four-block plan book, especially with seven class periods of instruction. (How bizarre!) To this day, most plan books have not been redesigned in over four decades and can't possibly work in today's world. Everyone complains about it, more often than not filling it out with fictitious lesson plans because it just doesn't work. The happiest schools are the ones not required to turn in plans at all, which presents another problem. I didn't say *most functional,* just happy not to be micromanaged.

It was during my first year that I created my own planner out of simple necessity. The need to succeed made me immediately change the system I was initially introduced to! I will share with you how to create this long-term planner in the next chapter. When completed, you will share your plans and how they fit into this year's Calendar with all your students. A Countdown will be part of your planning process and the classroom Calendar, which will also include all of the events taking place in your room. Your students will enjoy knowing what standards they will be responsible for mastering each quarter. They will also have a visual awareness of the upcoming deadlines because so much of what matters will now be on the Calendar that they scan frequently.

A Countdown, indicating how much time is left, is a very helpful and new motivator for most students. For example, on the second day of school there is a small 179/139 placed next to the date, which means that there are 179 days of school left, but only 139 days to learn everything that needs to be learned. Calendars help students in all grade levels who are not time sensitive to realize how many days have already been used up and how many are left until that midterm or book report is due. Countdowns enable students in every area to create self-motivating deadlines that inspire them to get moving. Having the school year and their standards-driven workload broken up into brain-compatible chunks gives students new beginnings and fresh starts far more frequently than ever before.

## Curves

Total Teachers use the Curve strategy to help students visualize their progress. Here is how you begin. On the board, simply draw a basic Curve that looks like this.

You will be using this type of Curve *all the time*! Next you say something like:

Ladies and gentlemen, how many of you have ever been to a major department store in your area? [*All hands go up; you now have them all on the same page.*] Now let me ask how many of you have ever been there early on a rainy weekday morning?

Probably no hands will go up, so put a zero at the far left end of the Curve.

Now how many of you have ever been shopping at that store on a sunny Saturday afternoon?

Probably most of the class will raise their hands.

Let's say there were about 100 shoppers in the store on a busy day.

Put that number on the far right-hand side of the Curve.

In the world of business it is important to keep track of lots of data, including how many shoppers the business expects to get. Depending on how much business they expect to have, they will know how many registers to open, the number of people to have on the floor, how often the bathrooms must be cleaned, and other things. When a place of business sells lots of merchandise and the employees are all being very productive, they turn a profit.

This is a good place to stop and explain what "profit" means. Emphasize how important math is in the world of business.

Who knows some of the times of the year when a retail store may have to gear up for extra business? . . .

That's right, before school begins, before holidays like Easter, Halloween, Christmas, and Valentine's Day, and times like that. Those are not average weeks. They are above average. Who can explain what "average" means? . . .

What do I mean when I say "business was average"? ...

Now think about owning a store, would you want business to be just average? ...

What about the people you hire. Would you want average people working for you, or would you raise the bar by hiring above-average employees?

I cannot drive home the importance of this lesson enough. You can make it age appropriate, but every grade level will devour this tool. All students enjoy the scenario because it is empowering, engaging, and very personal. Few students want to view themselves as average, and they need to know that, with a little effort, they can strive to be above average, and together they can bring up the average of the entire class. When the Curve concept is presented and used consistently at their level, it becomes a very constructive and informative tool. This is why it must be presented in an extremely grown-up fashion, even at the lowest of elementary levels. We all know we can be successful, provided we know where we are going, how and when we will get there, and believing that we *can* get there!

Wow those interpretations were great. I believe you really do understand what I mean about the right end of the Curve being the way above average side, being super terrific. The left side of the Curve, on the other hand, is quite unprofitable. It's slow, there's no business, but that's not necessarily a bad thing. It's where we usually begin. Most businesses don't do super well when they first open. The problem is if you stay at the left end of the Curve and don't improve.

OK now let's look at the middle of the Curve. You can see that average is just as far from the bottom as the top.

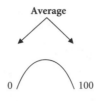

The average days are the days when there is no mad rush, no great sale or special event, but there aren't no customers in the store either. It's just a typical day.

Ladies and gentlemen, we are going to use this Curve a great deal in our classroom. It will show us honestly where we are so that we can help each other and ourselves. I've already told you that in this class it is perfectly all right to make mistakes, just as long as you learn from those mistakes. How will we keep track of knowing whether we're learning from our mistakes? You are certainly grown-up enough to know that if you did not do well on a quiz and are still on the left side of the Curve, you need to take it upon yourself and do some very intensive studying so that you do not hold up your class.

Here's how the Curve will help us. When you do an assignment, your grade—not your name, just your grade—will get posted on the Curve. When you look at the grade on your paper, you will be able to see how you rank in the class. Let's look up here at my class's grade point average, or GPA, from last year and the improvements they made in just two weeks.

Here you should explain what a grade point average is and how it is calculated. Even little children understand a team effort and acronyms. It's part of their world. This is an ideal time to teach them (way ahead of schedule) how to average grades, prices, or even temperatures for the month. These are first-grade subjects taken to third- or fourth-grade comprehension almost immediately! A GPA exemplifies teamwork, something they love!

Now quite frankly I think you can and will have a higher GPA than what I will show you now. Let's make that our class goal: to obtain a higher GPA than my class last year. You will definitely help me out here because I have to show AYP. That means annual yearly progress.

Here is a great example of an actual Curve. The date was January fifth, right after winter break. The teacher was not pleased and neither were the students! The class was tested again on January twenty-first. Look at how much they improved. The class GPA increased over thirteen points. Just two weeks later the class GPA went up another thirteen points!

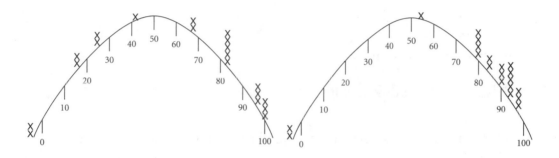

Wow! This is most impressive! This is how one of my students explained what our Curve tells us.

Below Basic is the far left side, and that is when we don't know something yet. Basic is near the top of the left side, and that is where our grades show up when we know things just a little. When we are Proficient, we are over the hump. We see our grades near the top on the right side of the Curve. Proficient means we know things fairly well. But the really great place to be is in the right-hand bottom corner because that means we really understand something. We are Advanced!

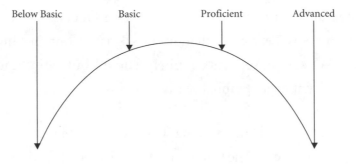

For a change, the Curve can sometimes be divided this way:

• Below Basic: "Don't know it yet."

• Basic: "Sort of know it."

• Proficient: "I know it."

• Advanced: "I really know it!"

There are many ways to implement the Curve concept in your class-room. One way is to laminate one and display it. Or get a flip chart and make them daily, allowing you and the students to check for understanding and see their daily improvements. And, trust me, there will be so many improvements! They will gather around these graphs discussing how they can do better next time, pulling out papers, and asking each other for input. The responsibility becomes theirs, not yours. You can't make children do things they don't want to do. They *want* to see their grades on the right side of that Curve, and they know it is up to them to make that happen. They now have a way to do that successfully. They feel special, really admired, and smart. See Figure 1.2.

Figure 1.2 The Curve displays.

## Clocks

Once we know where we are going, we need to know how much time we have to get there! We adults often assume that our students think about so many things that we take time sensitivity for granted, but they do not. The fact that everyone has just twenty-four hours in a day to do everything that needs to be done is some-thing our students rarely think about. So it's important to get students to focus on the twenty-four-hour Clock.

Some teachers feel time sensitivity is so important that they introduce it during the first week of school. Figure1.3 is a look at how one teacher intro-duced the twenty-four-hour Clock. She began with our very basic twenty-four-hour Clock and added labels, as well as military time.

Figure 1.3 One teacher's twenty-four-hour Clock.

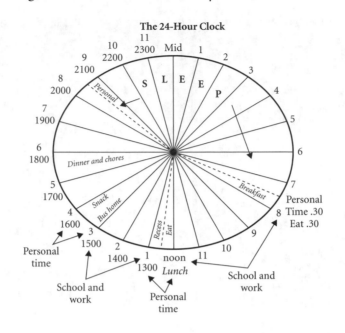

You'll have to explain military time and how that works. More prior knowledge will surface because some of your students will already be familiar with military time. This concept may lend itself to a wonderful discussion about time zones, Greenwich mean time, and more, making this a very enjoyable lesson.

With this type of participation, the students get involved and interested, thinking in new ways about time allocation and how it affects people and places everywhere. They also realize that collectively they know so much more, truly encouraging teamwork! Immediately they engage in conversation about free time, time at work, and time in bed. This is where still another discussion usually takes place: realizing that once a day is over, it is gone, never to be experienced again.

Ladies and gentlemen, let's look at these hours of our day, and think for a moment how they are spent. Let's look at eight to nine in the evening and brainstorm. What would be the best way to spend the hour or so before bed?"

You are looking for some personal reflections about the next day such as:

- Make sure everything is in my backpack for the next day *without* my mom or dad having to do it for me!

- Do I need to ask mom or dad to sign anything? If I do, I should remember to approach them with the paper and a pen!

- Perhaps review some of the material I know we will be addressing tomorrow.

- It's a good time to pick out my clothes, straighten up my room, and maybe go back out and spend some time with my family.

(You may want to make a list of these comments on the board.)

Of course, if it's the night of a scheduled ballgame or practice, things will be somewhat different, but you get the picture: Making use of productive time rather than squandering it away is important. This is a great place to share some interesting trivia, such as Tiger Woods' practicing golf between five and eight hours daily in order to be as good as he is. Engage the class in the comprehension of this concept:

So much is experienced if you play ball rather than if you simply watch someone else play ball. So let's make a conscious choice right now how to be the best that we can be, to utilize each and every day as a special gift. That is why it is called the "present." Let's make the most out of every one of the twenty-four hours that we are given because each hour is a gift!

So many teachers begin the year reviewing what they feel should have been taught last year. Much time is wasted, and many don't even realize how crucial the first two weeks are.

Goals need to be common, discussed, and monitored with instruments of accountability for

- *Short-term goals* (the twenty-four-hour Clock)

- *Intermediate goals* (Calendars, Countdowns, and Curves)

- *Long-term goals* (cumulative folders)

...

From the very beginning of your school year you will stress that you will present the material in a unique and complete fashion, to the best of your ability, enjoying student's relevant input. They will quickly realize that when they are not in attendance they miss the show, they miss the performance, and they miss a great deal that simply can't be made up with the same wonderful excitement that brought it center stage for the first time. Realizing this makes them not want to miss a single day of school. Like a great soap opera, you close each day with a cliff hanger that makes them look forward eagerly to the next episode.

It's time for these new tools and techniques to complement your new thinking, and now you know just how to get some of that accomplished. As you introduce these strategies to your students month by month, you will soon be gratified to see how they exceed all of your expectations!

# The Total Teacher Plan

## *A New Approach to Those 180 Days*

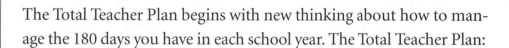

The Total Teacher Plan begins with new thinking about how to manage the 180 days you have in each school year. The Total Teacher Plan:

- Outlines where you are going and how to get there.

- Is shared with your students, who will work diligently for their teacher and for themselves as total students.

- Models the world of business and helps creates a desirable work ethic, instilling the want to work in students.

- Creates classrooms that are filled with visually motivating tools, such as Clocks, Curves, Countdowns, Calendars, and self-directed strategies, such as Teach it, Transfer it, Test it, and Apply it to the adult world (TTTA), all of which help students master standards and stimulate self-motivation.

- Is standards based and student centered to intrinsically motivate total students.

# The Typical School Calendar

*L*et's start by looking at the typical school calendar in Figure 2.1. A typical school calendar has the items shown in Figure 2.2 (which are also indicated in the Total Teacher Plan).

Many variations of school calendars are available today. Some schools are year-round, others function with ninety-minute blocks and alternative day scheduling. Other schools are traditional with forty-five-minute class periods. Some schools have miniclasses that last only forty-five days. Other schools have limited special areas allowing those teachers to meet with their students only once a week. There are many variations of daily schedules, but all students are required to attend school 180 times each year

All school calendars share several common components:

- They consist of 180 days for teachers to interact with students. Just recently schools in trouble have been extended to 200 or 225 days. If you are on an extended schedule simply add the additional days to your review time.

- Teacher workdays are to be spent in their rooms working.

- Professional development days are for ongoing teacher training.

- Progress (interim) reports and report cards are issued to parents.

- *Most* districts issue report cards every nine weeks, some every six weeks.

- Workdays, holidays, early release days, and vacations days vary.

The problem with traditional planners and pacing guides is that they are based on having 180 days, but teachers never really have that number

## Figure 2.1 A typical school calendar.

| August | | | | |
|---|---|---|---|---|
| **M** | **T** | **W** | **TH** | **F** |
|  |  | 1 | 2 | 3 |
| 6 R | 7 W | 8 W | 9 W | 10 R |
| 13 W | 14 W | 15 W | 16 W | 17 W |
| 20 ✗ | 21 | 22 | 23 | 24 |
| 27 | 28 | 29 | 30 | 31 |

| September | | | | |
|---|---|---|---|---|
| **M** | **T** | **W** | **TH** | **F** |
| 3 H | 4 | 5 | 6 | 7 |
| 10 | 11 | 12 | 13 | 14 |
| 17 | 18 | 19 | 20 | 21 |
| 24 | 25 | 26 | 27 | 28 |
|  |  |  |  |  |

| October | | | | |
|---|---|---|---|---|
| **M** | **T** | **W** | **TH** | **F** |
| 1 | 2 | 3 | 4 | 5 |
| 8 | 9 | 10 | 11 | 12 |
| 15 | 16 | 17 | 18 | 19 |
| 22 ✹ | 23 Q | 24 | 25 | 26 |
| 29 | 30 | 31 RC |  |  |

| November | | | | |
|---|---|---|---|---|
| **M** | **T** | **W** | **TH** | **F** |
|  |  |  | 1 ER | 2 |
| 5 | 6 | 7 | 8 | 9 |
| 12 H | 13 | 14 | 15 | 16 |
| 19 | 20 | 21 R | 22 H | 23 H |
| 26 | 27 | 28 | 29 | 30 |

| December | | | | |
|---|---|---|---|---|
| **M** | **T** | **W** | **TH** | **F** |
| 3 | 4 | 5 | 6 | 7 |
| 10 | 11 | 12 | 13 | 14 |
| 17 | 18 | 19 ER | 20 V | 21 V |
| 24 H | 25 H | 26 H | 27 V | 28 V |
| 31 V |  |  |  |  |

| January | | | | |
|---|---|---|---|---|
| **M** | **T** | **W** | **TH** | **F** |
|  | 1 | 2 | 3 | 4 |
| 7 | 8 | 9 | 10 | 11 Q |
| 14 ✹ | 15 | 16 | 17 | 18 |
| 21 H | 22 | 23 RC | 24 ER | 25 |
| 28 | 29 | 30 | 31 |  |

| February | | | | |
|---|---|---|---|---|
| **M** | **T** | **W** | **TH** | **F** |
|  |  |  |  | 1 |
| 4 | 5 | 6 | 7 | 8 |
| 11 | 12 | 13 | 14 | 15 |
| 18 V | 19 ✹ | 20 | 21 | 22 |
| 25 | 26 | 27 | 28 |  |

| March | | | | |
|---|---|---|---|---|
| **M** | **T** | **W** | **TH** | **F** |
|  |  |  |  | 1 |
| 4 | 5 | 6 | 7 | 8 |
| 11 | 12 | 13 | 14 | 15 |
| 18 ✹ | 19 | 20 | 21 | 22 Q |
| 25 | 26 | 27 | 28 | 29 RC |

| April | | | | |
|---|---|---|---|---|
| **M** | **T** | **W** | **TH** | **F** |
| 1 H | 2 V | 3 V | 4 V | 5 V |
| 8 | 9 | 10 ER | 11 | 12 |
| 15 | 16 | 17 | 18 | 19 |
| 22 | 23 | 24 | 25 | 26 |
| 29 ✹ | 30 |  |  |  |

| May | | | | |
|---|---|---|---|---|
| **M** | **T** | **W** | **TH** | **F** |
|  |  | 1 | 2 | 3 |
| 6 | 7 | 8 | 9 | 10 |
| 13 | 14 | 15 | 16 | 17 |
| 20 E | 21 O | 22 G T | 23 | 24 |
| 27 H | 28 | 29 | 30 | 31 |

| June | | | | |
|---|---|---|---|---|
| **M** | **T** | **W** | **TH** | **F** |
| 3 | 4 ER ✗ | 5 Q | 6 W R | 7 R |
| 10 | 11 | 12 | 13 | 14 |
| 17 | 18 | 19 | 20 | 21 |
| 24 | 25 | 26 | 27 | 28 |
|  |  |  |  |  |

Figure 2.2 Items in a typical school calendar.

| | |
|---|---|
| ✗ | First and last days of school year |
| Q | End of nine weeks |
| W | Workday-mandatory |
| H | Teacher holiday |
| ▩ | No school for students |
| R | Workday—optional |
| V | Vacation day |
| ✱ | Workday—set as W or R by individual schools |
| RC | Report cards are sent home |
| ER | Early release day for students (three hours early) |

**Report Cards:**
Report Cards are due six working days after the end of the grading period.

**Makeup Days:**
Student Makeup Days will be scheduled on Teacher Workdays as needed.

**Early Release Days:**
Individual schools will add one additional Early Release Day.

of days to actually do their jobs: hurricanes, snow days, fire drills, guest speakers, and many other time-stealing situations take away a number of those days.

Also, curriculums written based on 180 days often conflict with what is already in place in a given district. Scripted programs and pacing guides are usually written by people other than the teacher, leaving very little room for teachable moments, creativity, or the various culturally diverse needs that must be dealt with and often cannot be predicted. When a pacing guide is not created by the teachers performing the instruction, it is often in conflict with things like teacher style or geographic requirements.

*Bottom line:* We do *not* have 180 days to complete the task of teaching and reviewing the standards prior to students being tested on the ones that have been mastered. In reality, teachers have fewer than 140 days to teach and introduce the state standards. The rest of the time is needed to review the material prior to the standardized state tests and for students to comprehend all the material and learn to apply it successfully.

# Organization of the Plan

The Total Teacher Plan allows for students to internalize and understand the standards and for teachers to have the ability to teach to completion within the parameters of a doable (and enjoyable) schedule. In the Total Teacher Plan, we count down to those ever so important exams, the state standardized tests. We stay constantly aware of how much time is left to get the job done in a capable, stress-free fashion. We now have a tool that allows us to view these requirements with an exciting new awareness of time.

The plan is organized in five-week blocks because typically after the first five weeks, interim progress reports are sent home, then after the next four or five weeks, report cards go home. The first two marking periods are spent learning and understanding the standards. The third marking period becomes an exciting one, because two-thirds of the standards have already been mastered with only one-third to go. Never before have you or your students been this far along this early in the school year.

The reason is that everyone is working together to meet the deadlines outlined at the onset of the school year. Deadlines motivate all of us: tax time, paycheck time, vacation time. We all eagerly work toward deadlines when we are aware of them; a missing link in today's classroom is not having the right tools in order to do the job right. We know the work that needs to be accomplished. We become far more comfortable, capable, and confident when we know where we are going, how and when we will get there and what is expected! Some of your new tools are the twenty-four-hour Clock and the thinking it generates, the Calendars for the visual learners, the Curves for the competitive student, knowing how to TTTA (teach, transfer, test, and apply) for the self-starter, and homemade notebooks for note taking that inspire those who just would not take notes in the past.

The fourth marking period brings with it a great feeling that everyone is now very prepared and ready to go over any and all materials with a new developmentally appropriate series of questions and comments. The class functions as a winning team. If someone is dropping the ball or having difficulty with a particular process, it is no longer a bad situation. It's simply situational awareness, and any number of team players will gladly work their strengths in conjunction with the weakness of others to create a win/win scenario that elevates all involved. You, the teacher, deserve a big Ta Da! By remembering the wise words of Gandhi, "We must be the change we want to see," you have led a team with the expertise of a world-class change agent. You have modeled an I-can attitude, feeling very sure about everyone's ability, and the success of your team reflects the old adage: Anything the mind can conceive and believe, it can achieve.

## Setting Up Your Total Teacher Planner

The Total Teacher Planner is like a recipe that gives you the basic timing and ingredients but that leaves room for lots of those creative shifts that can continually add spice and variety. Let's take a look at how it is broken down. Each page in the planner holds five weeks in total, as shown in Figure 2.3. Figure 2.4 shows the plan for one week in March, and Figure 2.5 shows the plan for the first two weeks of school. Above the days of the week is where you place the Countdown. Your after-school commitments should be entered at the bottom of the page.

Figure 2.3 A blank planner page.

**The Total Teacher® Planner**

**1st Quarter, Part I**

| | Mon | Tue | Wed | Thu | Fri | Mon | Tue | Wed | Thu | Fri | Mon | Tue | Wed | Thu | Fri | Mon | Tue | Wed | Thu | Fri | Mon | Tue | Wed | Thu | Fri |
|---|---|---|---|---|---|---|---|---|---|---|---|---|---|---|---|---|---|---|---|---|---|---|---|---|---|
| # of Days to Teach | 140 | 139 | 138 | 137 | 136 | 135 | 134 | 133 | 132 | 131 | 130 | 129 | 128 | 127 | 126 | 125 | 124 | 123 | 122 | 121 | 120 | 119 | 118 | 117 | 116 |
| # of Days in Attendance | 179 | 178 | 177 | 176 | 175 | 174 | 173 | 172 | 171 | 170 | 169 | 168 | 167 | 166 | 165 | 164 | 163 | 162 | 161 | 160 | 159 | 158 | 157 | 156 | 155 |
| | 8/31 | 9/1 (Sep) | 9/2 | 9/3 | 9/4 | 9/7 | 9/8 | 9/9 | 9/10 | 9/11 | 9/14 | 9/15 | 9/16 | 9/17 | 9/18 | 9/21 | 9/22 | 9/23 | 9/24 | 9/25 | 9/28 | 9/29 (Oct) | 9/30 | 10/1 | 10/2 |

**Subjects and Times**

**After School (or cut and paste your schedule)**

**Notes**

- Week 1
- Week 2
- Week 3
- Week 4
- Week 5

Figure 2.4 A planner page for a week in March.

## Weekly Planner

| Subjects and Times | MON 3/6 | TUE 3/7 | WED 3/8 | THU 3/9 | FRI 3/10 | To Do List |
|---|---|---|---|---|---|---|
| Home Room PE | Planning | | | | | |
| Math 9:00–10:00 | Do word problems—in partners, cover ALL word problems in chapter | in WB—All odd then discuss pop quiz—trade and correct | Dare Do math 1/2 of next period Math review page | Go over yesterday's paper questions or comments. Pick items out of jar + estimate their length —end with sharing | Take class outside and pace off "All things in Area" learn to estimate school buses, etc. using yards | |
| Break | Break | Break | Break | Break | Break | |
| Lit 10 + 5 + L/A 12:15 | Read and Discuss | Shimmershine Queen | Compare characteristics in this week's story to Roll of Thunder | Discuss and compare papers | Write a clarification paper w/3 characteristic traits on any character so far. | |
| | Mon and Tues | 12–12:15 Read aloud Roll of Thunder and take notes on each chapter | | | 11:30 ART 12:15 | |
| AR + Lunch 12:15 | Lunch | Lunch | Lunch | Lunch | Lunch | |
| SS 1:20–2:00 | Guidance | Compare Canada's economy to that of Mexico | Quiz on state capitals and discuss current health problems in each region | Complete 2–3 min. oral reports on Mexico's economic concerns | Discuss current events based on Tuesday's economy discussion | |
| SC 2:00–2:35 | Read about the 6 Biomes | | Use const. paper and creatively write adjectives for each Biome fold into 6 sections | Discuss findings so far | Finish Biome chart and flower sketch | |
| 2:35–3:00 | | MUSIC | | | | |
| End of Day After School | Faculty Meeting Tutor after school 3–4:30 | | Parent conference | Tutor 3–4:30 | | |

Figure 2.5 Planner for first two weeks of school.

**1st Quarter, Part I**

| | | 8/6 | 8/7 | 8/8 | 8/9 | 8/10 | 8/13 | 8/14 | 8/15 | 8/16 | 8/17 | Notes |
|---|---|---|---|---|---|---|---|---|---|---|---|---|
| # of Days to Teach | X | | 179 | 178 | 177 | 176 | 175 | 174 | 173 | 172 | 171 | |
| # of Days in Attendance | X | | 140 | 139 | 138 | 137 | 136 | 135 | 134 | 133 | 132 | |
| | | | TUE | WED | THU | FRI | MON | TUE | WED | THU | FRI | |

**Subjects and Times**

| | TUE 8/7 | WED 8/8 | THU 8/9 | FRI 8/10 | MON 8/13 | TUE 8/14 | WED 8/15 | THU 8/16 | FRI 8/17 | Notes |
|---|---|---|---|---|---|---|---|---|---|---|
| Home room 8:00–8:15 | | | | | | | | | | Week 1 |
| PE 8:15–9:50 | | | | | | | | | | |
| Math 9:50–10:00 | PG 135–140 | | Chapter 11 PG 1412 review 146 | Quiz | PG 160–161 | Chapter 12 PG 162–172 | PG 173–190 | Pairs review | Quiz | Week 2 |
| Break 10:00–10:15 | | | | | | | | | | Week 3 |
| Computer 10:15–10:45 | | | | *Weekend* | | | | | | |
| SCHOOL 4A 10:45–11:30 | Spelling | nouns PG 210–212 | PG 215–230 | Send letters | VOCaB | | | | Spell Quiz | |
| Reading 11:30–12:45 | VOCaB | Read Klondike | A R T | | | Read Eisenstein | | | A R T | Week 4 |
| Lunch 12:45–1:15 | | | | | | | | | | |
| Vary: 1:20–2:00 T–Health W SS M1TH SC F SS | | SS N e Reagan | SC PGS 65–75 | SS NE States | SC PG 80–90 | | SS SE Reagan | SC pages 91–105 | SS SE states | Week 5 |
| 2:00–2:45 M W F Current T TH Events Writing | ♪ Music | C/e A–J | Paper on weather | C/e J–Z | C/e | ♪ Music | C/e | Make poster | C/e | |
| 2:45–3:00 Organization | 2:15–3:00 | | Study + Organize | | | 215–300 | Study + Organize | | | |

**After School (or cut and paste your schedule)**

Providing your students with a copy of the standards in brain-compatible chunks is how we begin. The material can easily be divided into thirds, just as marking periods are divided into fourths. Giving students only one-third of the standards at a time makes dealing with them doable rather than overwhelming.

The first third of the standards are handed out on the first day of school. During the initial forty-five days of a traditional school calendar, this preliminary third of the required material will be talked about, reworded, understood, applied, and mastered, hopefully by the time report cards go home. Then we wipe the slate clean; the first marking period is over. This becomes a sigh of relief for the students who perhaps were not as diligent and now realize they have a second chance at success.

The second nine weeks are spent on the next third of the state standards. This brings us to Winter break, the halfway mark of a school year, with two-thirds of the state standards already taught!

In January the teaching is centered around the last third of the state standards. The goal of dealing with all the standards a little before spring break will be accomplished. Students now have the opportunity to go over everything that has been introduced and discussed for another seven to eight weeks prior to taking a successful state exam.

In the event you are a teacher who has the students for only a semester (for just ninety days rather than the 180 days of a full year), the process is similar. The standards are still divided in thirds, allowing approximately 22 days to cover each third, with about twenty days left to review prior to midterms or finals. Some courses are taught for only forty-five days. These mini-courses are often not standards based, but the division of labor and review can be the same, keeping everyone focused with eleven days spent teaching each third of the material and about ten days before testing to review.

The ideal time to start your planning is at the end of the previous school year when everything is fresh in your mind. But let's assume that you have just gotten a job, and it's time to get busy. Having the planner on CD will make turning in plans very easy. Now is the time to actually make it happen for you. All summer you have thought about countless neat things to do. Close the door to your room, and let's begin. Remember that the beauty of this plan is that it is a work in progress.

Start by laying out the entire year, in the way that you truly *think* it will unfold. Then as your new thinking shifts, so will your strategies, generating new and far more successful results. Your students will help you keep the pace. When they do, you will become the sticky note superstar! You will simply slap a sticky note on top of your existing plan if you chose to print out your plan from the disk and have a hard copy on or desk, (or highlight the new idea electronically). This will give you the ability always to look at what you *thought was going to work* compared to what really worked and how you altered it. This wonderful work in progress will be worth its weight in gold as you begin your second year with this planner. You simply look back and capture everything that you did during year one: what (you thought) you were going to do but didn't, what worked and what didn't, how you tweaked things, and what you will do now.


## A Few Sample Planners

Let's look at a few examples of what completed planners look like.

Look at Figure 2.6. Down the left-hand side are the subjects being taught, with no space wasted for lunch or specials or planning. These activities require no planning on your part, you usually simply take your students to PE, Media, Lunch, or wherever; so a very thin line, indicating that these sessions are taking place, is all that is necessary. You will want the extra space for details about the subjects you are teaching. This is an elementary-level, self-contained teacher's plan, where one teacher teaches all the subjects. Across the top, above the month and date, are the days of the week plus the

Figure 2.6 A page in an elementary-level planner.

The Total Teacher® Planner

**1st Quarter, Part I**

| | Mon | Tue | Wed | Thu | Fri | Mon | Tue | Wed | Thu | Fri | Mon | Tue | Wed | Thu | Fri | Mon | Tue | Wed | Thu | Fri | Mon | Tue | Wed | Thu | Fri | Notes |
|---|---|---|---|---|---|---|---|---|---|---|---|---|---|---|---|---|---|---|---|---|---|---|---|---|---|---|
| # of Days to Teach | 140 | 139 | 138 | 137 | 136 | X | X | 135 | 134 | 133 | 132 | 131 | 130 | 129 | 128 | 127 | 126 | 125 | 124 | 123 | 122 | 121 | 120 | 119 | 118 | 117 | |
| # of Days in Attendance | 179 | 178 | 177 | 176 | 175 | X | X | 174 | 173 | 172 | 171 | 170 | 169 | 168 | 167 | 166 | 165 | 164 | 163 | 162 | 161 | 160 | 159 | 158 | 157 | 156 | |
| Subjects and Times | 8/31 (Sep) | 9/1 | 9/2 | 9/3 | 9/4 | 9/7 | 9/8 | 9/9 | 9/10 | 9/11 | 9/14 | 9/15 | 9/16 | 9/17 | 9/18 | 9/21 | 9/22 | 9/23 | 9/24 | 9/25 | 9/28 | 9/29 | 9/30 (Oct) | 10/1 | 10/2 | |
| MATH | Chapter 1 and 17 | | | | | xxx | Chapter 2 | | | | Chapter 3 | | | | | Chapter 4 | | | | | Chapter 5 | | | | | Week 1 |
| | | | | | | Labor Day | | | | | | | | | | | | | | | | | | | | |
| READING (enter time) | Nate the Great | | | | | | He Talks Twice | | | | Officer Buckle | | | | | Olympic Game | | | | | Basketball | | | | | Week 2 |
| LANGUAGE (enter time) | Sentences | | | | | | Statements | | | | Subject and Predicate | | | | | Compound subject and predicate | | | | | verbs / nouns / adverb / preposition / test | | | | | |
| SPELLING | Short a and e | | | | | Day OFF | Short i, o, u | | | | Long a and e | | | | | Long i, o, u | | | | | | | | | | Week 3 |
| SOCIAL STUDIES | State capitols | | | | | All week focus on state capitols | | | | | | | | | | | | | | | | | | | | Week 4 |
| SCIENCE | Explain how we will do labs | | | | | Outline the goal and what must be covered | | | | | Set up group | | | | | Plug in all work on big calendars | | | | | Make a pre quiz outline | | | | | Week 5 |
| After School (or cut and paste your schedule) | Faculty meets | | | | | Faculty meets | | | | | Faculty meets DDS | | | | | Faculty | | | | | Dinner with Dad | | | | | |

two Countdowns. This teacher uses the column on the right for notes and improvements week by week, and after-school commitments are included on the bottom.

In this first quarter of the year, the teacher decided to create a framework, with weekends boldly highlighted in yellow. This particular plan does not hold a lot of detail, simply the big picture. At a quick glance the teacher will be able to see where she wants to be five weeks from now when progress reports go home. The standards ought to be nearby where they can be easily accessed and crossed off as they are taught. During the first ten weeks you will be teaching the first third of the standards, and that is all you need to have at a time. You can go to the state website and cut and paste the standards into a working page that you can print them out for yourself and your students. The standards can also be broadly entered into the planner.

Figure 2.7 shows a high school or middle school planner where the teacher teaches three blocks and three subjects. Here the weekends are shaded, and the standards are cut and pasted to an attached page. This section represents a full marking period: nine or ten weeks, the entire first quarter.

As you can see, there is no right or wrong way to fill out these plans. Now that you will be able to do your plans electronically, it will be fun and easy. You'll find yourself cutting and pasting standards, clip art, and ideas. You'll have a much easier way to work with your plans than the initial teachers who had to do it all with pencils and highlighters. Design your plan so that it can capture everything, like a really great shopping list. You will be able to be as formal or as casual as you like. Some teachers want to make their planner pretty, interesting, cute, or subject specific using clip art or photos. Other teachers like to color-code their planners. Figure 2.8 shows a kindergarten teacher's planner for an entire year of very neat and organized plans.

Figure 2.7 A page in a high-school-level planner.

The Total Teacher® Planner

**1st Quarter Part I**

| | Mon | Tue | Wed | Thu | Fri | Mon | Tue | Wed | Thu | Fri | Mon | Tue | Wed | Thu | Fri | Mon | Tue | Wed | Thu | Fri | Mon | Tue | Wed | Thu | Fri |
|---|---|---|---|---|---|---|---|---|---|---|---|---|---|---|---|---|---|---|---|---|---|---|---|---|---|
| # of Days to Teach | 140 | 139 | 138 | 137 | 136 | x | 135 | 134 | 133 | 132 | 131 | 130 | 129 | 128 | 127 | 126 | 125 | 124 | 123 | 122 | 121 | 120 | 119 | 118 | 117 |
| # of Days in Attendance | 180 | 179 | 178 | 177 | 176 | x | 175 | 174 | 173 | 172 | 171 | 170 | 169 | 168 | 167 | 166 | 165 | 164 | 163 | 162 | 161 | 160 | 159 | 158 | 157 |
| Date (Sep / Oct) | 8/31 | 9/1 | 9/2 | 9/3 | 9/4 | 9/7 | 9/8 | 9/9 | 9/10 | 9/11 | 9/14 | 9/15 | 9/16 | 9/17 | 9/18 | 9/21 | 9/22 | 9/23 | 9/24 | 9/25 | 9/28 | 9/29 | 9/30 | 10/1 | 10/2 |

**Subjects and Times**

|  |  |
|---|---|
| WEB DESIGN — Time: 10:00 — Number of students: 22 students | 8/31: *Outline strategies for good designs*; 9/2: *Day OFF*; 9/7: *Labor Day*; 9/8: *intro ppt limits*; 9/14: *Set up teams for comp*; 9/21: *Begin project*; 9/28: *All items are due Friday* |
| ACCOUNTING II — Time: 11:00 — Number of students: 18 students | 8/31: *Begin ledgers*; 9/1–9/2: *Prob-b-1 prob-b-2 Excel spread sheet*; 9/7–9/8: *consumer spending* |
| ACCOUNTING 1 — Time: 1:00 — Number of students: 16 students | 8/31–9/1: *Intro basic accounting principles*; 9/8: *Begin dialogues in a new format*; 9/14: *It's all about profit and loss*; 9/21: *Bottom lines and the role of the CPA*; 9/28: *Intro chapters that correspond with the state standards* |
| After School (or cut and paste your schedule) | 9/2: Program advisory mtg; 9/9: staff mtg; 9/16: open house; 9/21: fbla state leadership rally |

**Notes**

- Week 1 — Time: 10:00 — Number of students 22 students
- Week 2 — Cut and paste standards for wk 2
- Week 3 — Cut and paste standards for wk 3
- Week 4 — Cut and paste standards for wk 4
- Week 5 — Cut and paste standards for wk 5
- Log standards that were easily mastered and ones that were difficult

Figure 2.8 A page in a kindergarten-level planner.

The Total Teacher® Planner

**1st Quarter, Part I**

| # of Days to Teach | 140 | 139 | 138 | 137 | 136 | X | 135 | 134 | 133 | 132 | 131 | 130 | 129 | 128 | 127 | 126 | 125 | 124 | 123 | 122 | 121 | 120 | 119 | 118 | 117 |
| --- | --- | --- | --- | --- | --- | --- | --- | --- | --- | --- | --- | --- | --- | --- | --- | --- | --- | --- | --- | --- | --- | --- | --- | --- | --- |
| # of Days in Attendance | 179 | 178 | 177 | 176 | 175 | X | 174 | 173 | 172 | 171 | 170 | 169 | 168 | 167 | 166 | 165 | 164 | 163 | 162 | 161 | 160 | 159 | 158 | 157 | 156 |
| (day) | Mon | Tue | Wed | Thu | Fri | Mon | Tue | Wed | Thu | Fri | Mon | Tue | Wed | Thu | Fri | Mon | Tue | Wed | Thu | Fri | Mon | Tue | Wed | Thu | Fri |
| (date) | 8/31 | Sep 9/1 | 9/2 | 9/3 | 9/4 | 9/7 | 9/8 | 9/9 | 9/10 | 9/11 | 9/14 | 9/15 | 9/16 | 9/17 | 9/18 | 9/21 | 9/22 | 9/23 | 9/24 | 9/25 | 9/28 | 9/29 | 9/30 | Oct 10/1 | 10/2 |
| **Subjects and Times** | | | | | | | | | | | | | | | | | | | | | | | | | |
| 8:30-9 Circle time | Calendar | | | | | Labor Day | Weather graph | | | | King and queen | | | | | Mom message | | | | | $$ and work | | | | |
| 9-10:10 Small Groups | Mon group 1 will dance | | | | | no kids day off | Mon | | | | Mon | | | | | Mon | | | | | Mon | | | | |
| 9-9:20 | Tues | | | | | | Tues | | | | Tues | | | | | Tues | | | | | Tues | | | | |
| 9:25-9:45 | Wed | | | | | | Wed | | | | Wed | | | | | Wed | | | | | Wed | | | | |
| 9:50-10:10 | Thurs | | | | | | Thurs | | | | Thurs | | | | | Thurs | | | | | Thurs | | | | |
| ROTATING GROUPS | Fri | | | | | | Fri | | | | Fri | | | | | Fri | | | | | Fri | | | | |
| 10:10-10:25 Shared reading | | | | | | | | | | | | | | | | | | | | | | | | | |
| 10:25 Wash hands | | | | | | | | | | | | | | | | | | | | | | | | | |
| 10:35 Lunch | | | | | | | | | | | | | | | | | | | | | | | | | |
| 10:50 Recess, Bathroom, $H_2O$ | | | | | | | | | | | | | | | | | | | | | | | | | |
| 11:30-12:15 Math/Science | | | | | | | | | | | | | | | | | | | | | | | | | |
| 12:15-1:00 Story/quiet time | | | | | | | | | | | | | | | | | | | | | | | | | |
| 1:30-2:00 Special Area: | Music | | | | | | | Computer | | | | | Art | | | | | Media | | | | | P E | | |
| 2:00-2:35 Snack and centers | | | | | | | | | | | | | | | | | | | | | | | | | |
| 2:45 DISMISS | | | | | | | | | | | | | | | | | | | | | | | | | |
| After school obligations or cut & paste your schedule | | | | | | | | | | | | | | | | | | | | | | | | | |

**Notes**

Wk 1 Our Presidents-
Letter of the week U u
Stories for each day will be:

Wk 2 DENTAL HEALTH WEEK
Letter of the week V v-
Stories for the week will be:

Wk 3 Celebrating Dr. Suess
Using all 5 senses
Monday: Cat in the Hat
Tuesday: Green Eggs and Ham
Wednesday, Thursday, Friday,

Wk 4 Fairy Tales
Learning the letter X x
Mon: Little Red Riding Hood
Tues: The 3 Little Pigs
Wed: Jack and the Beanstalk

A teacher who was going out on maternity leave, but she was completely relaxed about how things would go in her absence because she knew that her students would not miss a beat. Everything was outlined in perfect order in her planner right down to the standards, the specials, the times, and the after-school meetings. This page has a minute-by-minute schedule on the bottom left-hand corner, subjects down the left side, and the standards entered day by day.

Laying out and projecting your entire year for every one of the next 180 days may sound overwhelming, but it really is not—not if it is done in the way I am going to show you.

## Customizing Your Planner

Horizontally across the top of the planner are three Countdowns over the month and day of the week. First is the number of days remaining for you to teach the standards, and that begins with 140 on the first day. As we know, even though you have 180 days of school, you really only have 140 days to teach all of the standards, so that when you get to mid-March or early April with only 40 days left, they can be spent reviewing.

Your planner ought to be a reflection of you. Using certain colors for specific subjects or class periods allows you to make color-coded Curves for class competitions that complement the colors in your planner. If you enjoy stickers and clip art, use them. If you chose to print out your plans once you have them electronically created, you can add handwritten notes, or you can keep the planner on your computer and do it all electronically.

The important thing is that you have a planner in which can capture everything at all times and that gives you the flexibility to change and improve on things. It also lets you see your schedule in a five-week window, so you are always aware of where you are going and how much time you have to get there. Delete items or add notes so that next year you can make it that much better. Some teachers give a blank plan to their aides and have them use it to keep track of other things, such as attendance, interactions, parent pop-ins, or any number of things that complement your main planner.

## Incorporating the State Standards

Next let's look at what typical state standards look like when you get them. Here are some of the fourth-grade math standards for North Carolina.

The learner will read, write, model, and compute with nonnegative rational numbers.

The learner will understand and use perimeter and area.

The learner will recognize and use geometric properties and relationships.

The learner will understand and use graphs, probability, and data analysis.

The learner will demonstrate an understanding of mathematical relationships.

Develop number sense for rational numbers 0.01 through 99,999. a) Connect model, number word, and number using a variety of representations. b) Build understanding of place value (hundredths through ten thousands). c) Compare and order rational numbers. d) Make estimates of rational numbers in appropriate situations.

Develop fluency with multiplication and division: a) Two-digit by two-digit multiplication (larger numbers with calculator). b) Up to three-digit by two-digit division (larger numbers with calculator). c) Strategies for multiplying and dividing numbers. d) Estimation of products and quotients in appropriate situations. e) Relationships between operations.

Solve problems using models, diagrams, and reasoning about fractions and relationships among fractions involving halves, fourths, eighths, thirds, sixths, twelfths, fifths, tenths, hundredths, and mixed numbers.

As you can see, these standards appear to be complicated and lengthy. So let me now explain how this daunting task of teaching it all is made incredibly easy.

## Scheduling

There are only about thirty weeks (I refer to them as thirty Fridays) to complete your task of presenting and teaching a great deal of standards-based, and grade-level-appropriate material to twenty-five to thirty (elementary) or 150 or more (middle or high school) very different students. The completion of teaching your standards must meet a deadline, and that deadline is approximately six to eight weeks prior to the end of school. You and your students must get through understanding the standards in 135 to 140 days.

The first thing that must happen is this: Students must have a tangible copy of what they will be responsible for. They also must have a syllabus and calendars for them to see at all times. On the calendars will be your dual Countdown indication of how much time is left to learn and the actual days left in the school year.

You will be working to finish with sufficient time left for review before finals. You will need at least five to six weeks in a traditional schedule, and at least two weeks if you are working on a ninety-day semester schedule. If you only have seventy-five days to teach, you'll need about fifteen days of that to review.

One week for standardized testing must be filled into your planner. You will have those dates long before you have dates for anything else. So let's begin by turning to the last quarter and entering the test dates into May.

We then begin mapping out the standards, one-third at a time. Learning the standards will take up about twenty-seven weeks; then you review for about six weeks, leaving two weeks for testing and closing down shop. At this point, you are not yet entering anything academic in your planner at all.

Collect all nonacademic dates and deadlines.

- Have some fun entering things like your significant other's birthday, your doctors' appointments, and anything else that you already have set into your personal schedule that you want to organize around.

- Pick up the school calendar, and enter the dates for report cards, prescheduled workshops, meetings, optional and mandatory workdays, days off, early dismissals, and so on.

- Take out your personal date book and transfer anything of significance. Perhaps you tutor after school or teach at the university part-time. Plug those dates in now.

- You may be responsible for the cafeteria bulletin board or a luncheon once a quarter. Don't let these obligations creep up on you. Put them in the planner now. Chances are they won't change, and even if they do, it's easy to move them around.

- Take a few minutes more and scan your thoughts: birthdays, trips, or anything you know will be coming up can be entered now.

You won't believe how organized you'll feel the first time someone asks you whether you can do this or that and with a quick look at your planner you will be able to say yes or, "Sorry, I am all tied up that day." You will realize immediately whether you have to reschedule that first after-school meeting because it overlaps with your family reunion. Yes, you can have a life outside school, allowing for perfect balance. This process will make you feel so good, you may get lost in the fun of it all!

### Entering Academic Information

Vertically along the left-hand side of each page, place the subjects you teach. You will need to create horizontal lines to separate your classes. Entering the horizontal lines yourself allows you to personalize how you break up your pages based on the classes you teach. No two teachers' schedules are exactly the same, so no two planners will be the same. This is why the horizontal lines are not printed in advance, as in standard planners. The horizontal lines you insert can make the blocks as wide or as narrow as you like to suit your needs. You will be concentrating on your subjects, the actual classes you teach. If you teach math five periods each day, create five blocks, because each class may be at a different place. If you teach all subjects, you will have a plan that is divided in sections for:

- Reading/ English language arts/writing

- Math

- Science

- Social studies

- Plus any other subject that you teach such as current events, computer skills, etc.

You also have a section that runs along the bottom of every page for after-school commitments. Leaving the bottom of the page open for after-school obligations will make it easy for you to know at a glance whether you are free. So should a parent want to schedule a conference, you will know right away whether it will be convenient for you or not.

Each section of the planner contains five weeks, so you will know that each time you finish a section, either a progress report or a report card will be going home. Continue filling in your schedule for this year, setting up your Countdown and dates for the rest of the year, quarter by quarter on eight total pages, two per quarter.

(Before you continue, take a look at the next part of this section, where you are introduced to a miniplanner that will help you find inspiration and more planning ideas. Also browse through Section 3, on month-by-month ideas.)

You may also want to grab a student copy (not the teacher's edition) of any textbooks you use, in addition to the standards. Next to each group of standards or objectives, jot down which chapters of the textbooks reinforce them. Or you could also note the chapters in the planner on the day you will be covering that material. You will be able tell your students that their books have additional explanations of the standards and that they can refer to them if need be. The textbooks are also helpful for remedial work for students who don't master the skills as quickly as others. Parents also find the textbooks helpful to reinforce the standards. The standards are often confusing and difficult for parents, so knowing where to cross-reference standards to textbook pages becomes very helpful.

This planner will be your anchor and your reason for unbelievable success. You will finally have the time you need, as well as a way to implement all those wonderfully creative things you know will benefit your students. If there is not a plan in place for how you will get to where you are going, you probably won't get there.

Now look at the last day of school in your plan, and pace back six weeks. That is when you will begin reviewing; and that is when the schedule becomes most labor intensive for your students. Get familiar with the standards and begin grouping them logically, creating convenient stopping points, test dates, and project deadlines. For example, if you are going to teach language arts through your favorite novel, then divide the pages, and cross-reference them with the standards that you will cover. If you are using newspapers to teach math, think about your strategies.

I once worked with a science teacher who had to share lab equipment and time. She decided to teach all theory first, pretty much the way it's done in medical school; then, after all the standards were introduced and comprehended, she moved on to the experiments and labs. Her scores were the highest the district ever experienced. Will this work for everyone? Maybe not. But it certainly worked for her because she was comfortable with her decision, it fit well into her schedule, and she was able to motivate her students.

A good practice is to not give homework on a subject unless the standard is *not* mastered. If that is what you choose to do, then use workbook and textbook pages for these assignments. Pencil in pages and places where you can refer students who need extra help working with difficult standards.

Take a break. You are mapping out the entire year for the first time, and your plan is standards based and student centered. *Wow!* If this is the first time you have attempted to lay out the entire school year's obligations in one clean sweep, you need to be congratulated. This is different than collective long-range plans that get turned in to the office and are never seen or used again. This is your personal approach that you will keep and work from.

It will probably take you the better part of two or three full days, depending how much fun you are having, to accomplish the task of being on time and on top. Don't get discouraged if you have several ideas that don't pan out. You may crumple up several attempts and toss them, but that is a good thing because it proves that you are using that new thinking, and your thoughts are probably circulating all over the place. Just begin with a rough draft or even separate lists. Remember the Total Teacher-i*sm:*

> It is perfectly all right to make mistakes, provided we learn from those mistakes.

And that applies to teachers as well as to students. We all have great ideas that make us arrange and rearrange things differently from year to year, constantly improving our methods. *You* don't want to be the teacher who has "been teaching the same way for thirty years," do you?

By now you are probably rather excited about integrating some of the reading material with the math, and blending it all with the standards in science and social studies if you are self-contained. If you are departmentalized, I know your mind is buzzing with new ways to get it all introduced in an exciting fashion. One teacher put pockets on each printed-out planner page. She passed out the corresponding standards, then collected them after each student validated that those standards were mastered. Another teacher would not turn in her plans. She adamantly told the principal these are my plans and they belong on my desk for me to improve or import. If you want me to make you a copy I will, but they stay on my desk. He more than respected her commitment to her plan and came in from time to time to simply take a peek!

Let's look at a few things you may want to remember:

- Break up the schedule. Make stopping points logical.

- Keep the standards front and center. Remember that teaching them to mastery is the goal.

- Lay out your planner with lessons that can integrate all your subjects. For example, use lessons from social studies when wording math problems, and engage the students in sharing how the standards are applicable to their world.

- When you look at your planner, the spreadsheet for the quarter, your mind's eye will continuously focus on where you are going, while your actual eyes will see how much needs to be done, how you will teach the standards each day, and what areas or tools you will cover or use. You can make the planner as broad or as detailed as necessary for you.

- Use each Friday wisely, wrapping up what you've accomplished and setting goals for the following week. Perhaps quizzes, trivia, seat rotation based on increased GPAs, or even selective assignments for those who are interested. Remember that suggestions and choices generate more buy-in than demands and commands.

- Be creative when mapping out your methods. Feel free to blend standards and units or move them around. There will be very little homework until late in the year, but if a particular process requires it, just enter it into your plan.

- Design a method that checks off or highlights standards as they are introduced, taught, and mastered. This can save you tons of time if you transfer that job to your students, allowing them to check off what they have mastered. The more they interact with their list of standards, the more they will learn them. These tasks can be executed by the students because the planner has them front and center for you to deploy in a timely manner.

- Remind yourself to collect, save, then give back all work accumulated each quarter so that it can be personally used at review time.

- Make changes in the notes section frequently. For example, if you have always taught fractions prior to decimals, and this year realize that teaching decimal first really worked out more successfully, indicate that in the notes area. Or if you find great vocabulary words, jot them down for reference next year, along with new trivia.

- Use the notes area for all things that will improve your AYP (annual yearly progress), increase your GPA, or help in any fashion. Often a simple shift in the way certain standards are introduced, or in their sequence, can make monumental differences. In the past they may have been forgotten once they were used, so if you make notes in this section, post it on the page with a sticky note. The notes section tightens up and improves your techniques and strategies for the next year.

- Keep updating your after-school area, entering appointments or obligations as they happen.

- Think *documentation*. This planner will be the catch-all for not only teaching strategies and standards, but also for the documentation that is so vital in our profession. For example, let's assume that a particular student is exhibiting unusual behaviors. You have a perfect place each and every day to make very simple notes regarding the situation. The notes area is often extended by teachers with a foldout because it becomes an indispensable part of journaling what takes place, what works, and often what does not work for reference when planning for next year.

- A page at the end of the planner can be used for monthly summaries. Administrators really like that, and it is an excellent way for you to refresh your thoughts as you begin planning next year. (See Figure 2.9.)

- The other page at the end of the planner can be used to indicate your students' test scores from previous years and to compare them to the gains they make in your room by entering the names and grades in columns. Many educators fall short of meeting AYP, but you will smile with pride as you notice how many students ended the previous year at Below Basic and moved to enviable Proficient or Advanced placements under your direction. Principals are impressed when teachers use this page to keep a narrative of student progress. The end-of-grade test scores will no longer be stashed somewhere, hardly accessible; they will be right there, in your planner. (See Figure 2.10.)

Figure 2.9 End-of-month summaries.

## MONTH BY MONTH SUMMARY OVERVIEW OF MONTHLY EVENTS

**JUNE**

**JULY**

Completed plans for the year. My room looks great! Everything is ready so much earlier than ever before.

**AUGUST**

School began and the students loved the new format. New students were immediately paired up with students that have been here. Everyone got first third of the standards.

**SEPTEMBER**

By Labor Day we had our curves and calendars posted. Students love the four-question quiz.

**OCTOBER**

Everyone is writing their own progress report! They truly feel empowered with this new way of comprehending the state standards. Our GPA is 3.75!

**NOVEMBER**

We have begun the second third of the standards and are right on schedule. Holidays help with making standards applications real.

**DECEMBER**

The new way to approach the end of the first semester is working really well. We have learned 2/3 of the standards. Yay!

**JANUARY**

I gave the students a pop quiz on all they mastered the first 90 days. I am very pleased and so are they!!!

**FEBRUARY**

We are now counting down and the momentum is building. Everyone is learning and retaining information so we can ACE THE TEST!

**MARCH**

It's nearly time for spring break and we are almost done with all the standards! What a thrill. We will begin counting down to TEST TIME with great PLEASURE!

**APRIL**

The students, their parents, and I are so pleased. Finally a year when we knew where we were going and we got there! We are planning a field trip, so I'm glad I booked the buses back in August!!

**MAY**

The testing went great! I am ready for next year, the students made my new calendars and curves, and I am so excited. Having a TOTAL TEACHER YEAR is the best!

Figure 2.10 Progress sheet

| | PROGRESS SHEET | | | | |
|---|---|---|---|---|---|
| MEET AYP BY DOCUMENTING WHERE YOUR STUDENTS BEGIN AND WHERE YOUR STUDENTS CONCLUDE THE YEAR | | | | | |
| Students's Name | End of Grade Test Score from Previous Year (Below Basic, Basic Proficient, Advanced) | Subject | Mid Term Score | Final Exam | (+ or − point value) from Previous Year |
| EXAMPLE Anderson, Mary | Below Basic (1) | Math | Basic (2) | (3) Proficient | 2 |
| Tom Smith | Basic (2) | Math | Proficient (3) | (4) Advanced | 2 |
| Kaleb Collins | Basic (2) | Math | Advance (4) | (4) Advanced | 2 |
| Brittnay Kline | Proficient (3) | Math | Advance (4) | (4) Advanced | 1 |
| Sheila Green | Basic (2) | Math | Proficient (3) | (3) Proficient | 1 |
| | This documentation is easy to do and keeps track of the increases made by students,therefore meeting AYP Annual Yearly Progress | | | | |

- You may choose to give quizzes on Tuesdays, so perhaps highlight the top of every Tuesday with a particular color to remind you to begin with a pop four-question quiz.

- The planner becomes a partner, supporting continued improvement that comes across through increased student achievement and decreased workload for the teacher!

# The Total Teacher Miniplanner

*T*he miniplanner is another way to use the Total Teacher Planner. It is each teacher's own unique journal of things to say, things to think about, how to inspire, new things to do, and how to pace a student-centered, standards-based classroom. It's a reminder of the many possibilities that invite productive thinking, and it opens the doors for creating new and untapped potential in your students. It parallels the main Total Teacher planner in format, but unlike the main planner, the miniplanner is a thinking guide, a brief look at some of the new things you will be incorporating into your new mind-set.

Like the main planner, the miniplanner is organized in five-week increments, because after the first five weeks of school, most districts issue progress (interim) reports that must go home with the students. Four or five weeks after that, report cards go home, and then the first marking period is officially over. This process is repeated through the year.

There is a great deal to look over and comprehend in the miniplanner, so I'll give you a brief summary of each page.

## Sheet 1

The two rows of numbers that begin in the upper left-hand corner represent the two very important Countdowns that everyone in the class will be aware of at all times: the number of days left to teach and learn all the standards and the number of days actually in attendance. These series of numbers are directly above the day of the week and the date. When there is no school, there is no Countdown. For example, Labor Day, the first Monday of September, simply has an *X* to indicate that there is no time lost.

The sample miniplanner pages shown here (Figure 2.11) will give you an idea of how this can be used to schedule, record, and generate great ideas throughout the year. As you can see, this first sample page is full of suggestions. For example, good PR (public relations) is good business and will be worth the small amount of time it will take to accomplish. Calling all the parents soon after school starts is probably the best piece of positive public relations work you can do to begin promoting yourself and showing parents how different a teacher you are. No need to make it a lengthy conversation, and you don't need to speak to them directly either. You'll want to tell them (or leave a message that says) something like this:

> Mr. Smith, hello. This is Tommy's teacher; I just want to tell you what a pleasure it is to have your son in my class. He is a perfect gentlemen, and I so enjoyed getting to meet him. I am sure that we will have a delightful year. However, should anything take place that is less than pleasant, which I very seriously doubt, I will also call you then to keep you abreast of things.

You are certainly doing something that has rarely been done before. This probably very busy mom or dad came home to a positive and complementary message on their voicemail. What a nice surprise.

The miniplanner notes that you'll be passing out one-third of the state standards to all of your students as soon as possible. Students will quickly recognize that the language is confusing. You can change the language yourself into simpler questions, or you may let students work in groups to rewrite the standards in plainer language. There are any number of ways to change the language and make the standards more understandable and

Figure 2.11 Sheet 1 of the miniplanner.

| # of Days to Teach Info | 140 | 139 | 138 | 137 | 136 | 135 | 134 | 133 | 132 | 131 | 130 | 129 | 128 | 127 | 126 | 125 | 124 | 123 | 122 | 121 | 120 | 119 | 118 | 117 |
| # of Days in attendance | 179 | 178 | 177 | 176 | 175 | 174 | 173 | 172 | 171 | 170 | 169 | 168 | 167 | 166 | 165 | 164 | 163 | 162 | 161 | 160 | 159 | 158 | 157 | 156 |
| | M | T | W | Th | F | M | T | W | Th | F | X | M | T | W | Th | F | M | T | W | Th | F | M | T | W | Th | F |
| AUGUST | 20 | 21 | 22 | 23 | 24 | 27 Aug | 28 | 29 | 30 | 31 | x | 3 Sept | 4 | 5 | 6 | 7 | 10 | 11 | 12 | 13 | 14 | 17 | 18 | 19 | 20 | 21 |

**Subjects and Times**

Your Subject/ scheduled time will go here with appropriate personalized horizontal lines

Call every parent and tell them what a lovely child they have and what a pleasure it is to teach them. It's Good Business to begin that way

The Goal is ALWAYS the highest GPA ever!

Introduce T R J V J A about this holiday Why was there no school last Monday

Use your 24 hour clock— Pilots do! (no down time) (You can't afford it) Constantly jot things down in your big planner make it full of your big ideas

Pass out First 1/3 of the standards! Turn each one into a question and rewrite it on grade level. Let them know they must know them all in 40 more days chip away at it 1/3 at a time

You have approximately 30 Fridays to do a "Capable Job"

Use your big calendars—The business world does!

**After School (Or cut and paste your schedule)**

This is August. Read and apply the information in that chapter

Make the Deal Immediately - Go to Pg 12 - Min H.W. "if"

Progress Reports Go Home on "date"

**Notes**

Week 1 — Capture their interest- Did you know August is the only month with no holidays?

Week 2 — Talk about their cume folder—it validates what they do.

Week 3 — Teach probability by using a lottery seat exchange. They love it.

Week 4 — Clocks Calendars and Curves. Make it real!

Week 5 — Allow students to write their own Give them ownership over goals and responsibilities

1st Quarter

student friendly. Another idea is to use highlighters to group the standards that can be easily learned together.

By the fifth Monday, students can be writing their own progress reports and notes acknowledging what they are good at and where they need help. These student-generated evaluations can accompany your school-issued progress reports. They can say things such as, "Mom, I am really trying hard in my science class but not doing as well as I ought to be. I can teach some of the standards, and transfer them to my world but still have a hard time applying them to the adult world. Maybe you can help me with this."

## Sheet 2

The second page (Figure 2.12) tells us, that, when we are focused, we are less inclined to be discouraged (about our students), disappointed (about what is or is not taking place), or defeated (by the massive workload). When we share our focus with our students—many of us for the first time ever—they will become very clear about where everyone is going, when they will get there, what is expected, and why it is important.

This page also reminds us to take advantage of what's around us to come up with teachable moments. For example, did you know that "NEWS" stands for North, East, West, and South? Probably not, and neither did your students. Your classroom ought to have a clear indication of which wall is the North wall for internalizing a sense of direction. Even using online services such as Mapquest becomes easier when students can create a mental image of which way their classroom faces: north, south, east or west.

Everything on the walls ought to be of value, not simply decorative or convenient. October arrives and new interesting information ought to be introduced. Interesting trivia—such as the real definition of "googol" (an infinite number, not just a search engine) or why most fast-food chains use the color yellow in their logos (because yellow makes people hungry)—will

Figure 2.12 Sheet 2 of the miniplanner.

| # of Days Left TTT | | | | | | | | | | | | | | | | | | | | | | | | | | |
| # of Days Left | | | | | | | | | | | | | | | | | | | | | | | | | | |

| September | M | T | W | Th | F | | M | T | W | Th | F | | M | T | W | Th | F | | M | T | W | Th | F | Notes |
|---|---|---|---|---|---|---|---|---|---|---|---|---|---|---|---|---|---|---|---|---|---|---|---|---|
| | 116 | 115 | 114 | 113 | 112 | | 111 | 110 | 109 | 108 | 107 | | 106 | 105 | 104 | 103 | 102 | | 101 | 100 | 99 | 98 | 97 | Week 1 |
| | 155 | 154 | 153 | 152 | 151 | | 150 | 149 | 148 | 147 | 146 | | 145 | 144 | 143 | 142 | 141 | | 140 | 139 | 138 | 137 | 136 | |
| | 24 | 25 | 26 | 27 | 28 | Oct | 1 | 2 | 3 | 4 | 5 | | 8 | 9 | 10 | 11 | 12 | | 15 | 16 | 17 | 18 | 19 | |

Week 1 — Work your class or they'll work you!

Week 2 — Remember students take on the personalities of their teachers.

Week 3 — Plan your work. Work your plan.

Week 4 — If you don't know where you are going you won't get there.

Week 5 — Log the 1st benchmark on the last page; meet AYP.

1st Quarter

**Subjects and Times**

If you stay focused you won't be DISCOURAGED, DISAPPOINTED or DEFEATED

It's Autumn. What time does it officially happen?

Make "Your" place the place they will be hired or fired

Remember you are the CEO— will they be hired or fired

Talk about the business world

The One Rule
Effective communication is always kind, gentle, and respectful
It's the Rules of the Road in life that work!

Take advantage of stormy weather. Teach wind direction N-E-W-S use the weather page too.

EARLY DISMISSAL (vertical)

the end of quarter week day (vertical)

Benchmark test 1/3 of standards
45th Day

Report Cards Go Home

Seeing where you begin makes where you are headed special!

**After School** (Or cut and paste your schedule)

keep your students eager to learn. It is a wonderful classroom management tool. You can accumulate cool facts by asking for volunteers to research specific subjects. Your new tools will engage students in the act of learning more information on their own, and that enhances their comprehension.

Restated on this page, to remind yourself and your students to keep it in play, is the paramount classroom rule: Effective communication is always kind, gentle, and respectful.

Report cards go home at the end of the first nine-week period, and you will see that reminder at the bottom right-hand corner of the page. Reminders like this, or a brief nudge to plan your work and then work your plan, or a note that there is an early release next week, become instrumental in making you an outstanding Total Teacher. Seeing that you have introduced one-third of their required standards and students have mastered them by the time this report card goes home is more than motivating. Never before has this much been accomplished so early in the school year.

## Sheet 3

The third page (see Figure 2.13) shows that you have collected the first third of the standards, which have been highlighted (indicating what the students have either learned before), grouped together, or most recently mastered, and you have passed out the next third. Remember that we pass out the standards only one-third at a time at the beginning of each quarter. We also wipe the slate clean with this process, because if the students haven't mastered something, they will have an entire marking period to learn it again. They will be months older, developmentally wiser, and better able to digest this information, not for the first time, but at a better time. One teacher created four columns next to each standard, for Taught, Transferred, Tested, and Applied to the adult world, which allows students to keep track of what they have mastered.

Figure 2.13 Sheet 3 of the miniplanner.

| # of Days Left TTT | 92 | 91 | 90 | 89 | 88 | 87 | 86 | 85 | 84 | 83 | 82 | 81 | 80 | 79 | 78 | 77 | 76 | | 75 | 74 | 73 | 72 | 71 | Notes |
|---|---|---|---|---|---|---|---|---|---|---|---|---|---|---|---|---|---|---|---|---|---|---|---|---|
| # of Days Left | 131 | 130 | 129 | 128 | 127 | 126 | 125 | 124 | 123 | 122 | 121 | 120 | 119 | 118 | 117 | 116 | 115 | | 114 | 113 | 112 | 111 | 110 | Week 1 |
| October | M | T | W | Th | F | M | T | W | Th | F | M | T | W | Th | F | M | T | W | M | T | W | Th | F | |
| | 29 | 30 | 31 | 1 | 2 | Nov | 5 | 6 | 7 | 8 | 9 | Nov | 12 | 13 | 14 | 15 | 16 | 19 | 20 | 21 | 22 | 23 | 26 27 28 29 30 | |

**Subjects and Times**

Use → notes to indicate improvements
Year 1 Identify
Year 2 Rectify
Year 3 Fly

What will we learn?
Why must we learn it?
How will we use it?

Be creative with placement of standards

Rewrite each standard at your grade level.

**After School (Or cut and paste your schedule)**

---

**Week 1**

Let them teach. Empower them. To teach is to learn twice!

Refer to your 24 hour clock Work 8 Sleep 8 Play 8 a well rounded and balanced person

Notes: Feed Forward Feed Back—Do it

Keep the end in mind

**Week 2**

Read the November chapter and do the activities for next week's Thanksgiving assignment

Take the calendar down dramatically or cover it with standards mastered.

Notes: Cume folders track absences and behavior. Tell them "This is your job and you are being tracked"

Tiger Woods practices 8 hours everyday—share that

**Week 3**

Use calendars often. Remember students are not time sensitive and need the help

THANKSGIVING

x x x x x
x x x x x

Notes: Allow students to "Professionally evaluate you!" Empower them and learn from them.

**Week 4**

Pass out next 1/3 of the state standards and turn each one into a question

Patriotism is all about Respect, Discipline, and Pride. Read "Not Just a Children's Story" by Clavell out loud

Notes: Be enthusiastic "If you were a T.V. show, would you change the channel?"

**Week 5**

Let students create a test question and answer for each standard. Give out a syllabus

Tell a parent something positive.

Progress Reports Go Home

Notes: Let them write their own progress reports as if it were an employee evaluation

2nd Quarter

Winners Never Quit & Quitters Never Win

Always think ahead - That creates a win/win - not a win/lose or a lose/lose

Students are now data driven, which is a process that every district across America strives for but that most have not yet figured out how to do.

At review time you can pass the marked-up standards back to the students who own them. They love identifying what they have mastered and often say "Oh, I know this now!" Now your review is focused, relevant, and personal. No longer will the students who mastered all of the standards easily be bored to tears waiting for those who did not. Your class is easily motivated to use groups, levels, games, quizzes, reviews, and many other ways to TTTA all the standards.

The Countdown now indicates that by Thanksgiving there will be just about seventy-five days left to do your job, even though you will be coming to school for another 115 days. Remember that you are always in a dual Countdown, the number of days left until you begin your review (which is really the start of the last marking period) and the actual number of days left in the school year.

Veterans Day is also in November, and there are many ways to instill a sense of patriotism, community service, and pride in each student. Remember that discipline is behavior that requires no punishment, and the military is a fine example of outstanding, well-disciplined behavior. If you happen to be located near a military base, such as Paris Island in South Carolina, or Arlington Cemetery in Virginia, it can be a wonderful field trip.

Find a superstar (I happen to have chosen Tiger Woods for this mini-planner), and give your students a peek into the dedication that it takes to become the best at anything. Most students want to be things like professional basketball players or rock stars, but rarely do they realize the amount of hard work and dedication it takes to be the best. You can incorporate your twenty-four-hour clock when you explain that Tiger Woods practices for eight hours every day. It takes that kind of determination and desire to work hard, in order to be the best!

## Sheet 4

Sheet 4 takes us through winter break and the end of the first semester in January (see Figure 2.14). You will have many grade-filled bell Curves posted in your classroom. These Curves let your students see where they were at the beginning of the year and where they are now!

Another way to create valuable awareness in your students is to give them a midterm just prior to winter break and post the grades on a Curve. When the students return, give them the same test. There is often a surprising result for the students. Even after just a short two-week break, the scores can plummet, and the students can see this when the new grades are posted on the Curve. The students learn a valuable lesson: They had not learned the material for permanent recall. They will quickly alter their methods of retention, taking TTTA more seriously.

You are now at the halfway point of the traditional school Countdown, and you have already taught two-thirds of the standards with only one-third left to introduce. I am sure you already have a newfound attitude of gratitude knowing that this new school year can and will be different, especially because you will be ahead of schedule rather than running out of time!

## Sheet 5

The fifth page brings us through January and into February (see Figure 2.15). You will be aware of early dismissal days, Martin Luther King Jr. Day, President's Day, and other key dates for these five weeks. Standards become valid, and students become better educated when they not only honor Martin Luther King, Jr. but can teach someone about him and transfer his philosophies to their world. It's soon time for progress reports to once again go home.

Figure 2.14 Sheet 4 of the miniplanner.

# of Days Left TTT

| | | M | T | W | Th | F | | | M | T | W | Th | F | | | M | T | W | Th | F |
|---|---|---|---|---|---|---|---|---|---|---|---|---|---|---|---|---|---|---|---|---|

**# of Days Left TTT**: 70 69 68 67 66 / 109 108 107 106 105

**# of Days Left**: 65 64 63 62 61 / 104 103 102 101 100 ... 60 59 58 57 56 / 99 98 97 96 95 ... 55 54 53 52 51 / 94 93 92 91 90

December — DEC 3 4 5 6 7 — JAN 7 8 9 10 11 — 14 15 16 17 18

**Subjects and Times**

At the end of November share an "Attitude of Gratitude." You enjoy them!! It matters. Focus on winning. Be the class with the highest G.P.A. It's about teamwork

The Army/Navy game is a USA tradition. Predict the Outcome

Winter break begins on Friday

Did you make the December Gift they want to make? Read the December chapter

Who is playing in the Super Bowl? Where are those cities? Where will they play?

Read the January Chapter

EARLY RELEASE DISMISSAL

EARLY DISMISSAL

TEACHER WORKDAY

the year is half over…new semester begins on the next page

INSPIRE THEM
To teach is Not to learn
They must WANT to learn—we can't MAKE them learn!

No word rhymes with "orange."
It's a poet's nightmare

Tell a parent something positive

Fill in all After school Commitments too

**After School** (Or cut and paste your schedule)

Your students will become AWARE, HONEST, and RESPONSIBLE!
Teach comprehension a new way—use the economy
Report Cards
Go home next Friday

**Notes**

Assign the countdown to a student

**Week 1**
Jot down feedback—"Went well" or "Students did not enjoy lesson"

**Week 2**
Do the same bell curve test before and after break. If their grades drop they'll "see" it and internalize it. This is powerful.

**Week 3**
You've never been this far along or so organized, and they can feel it
2/3 Taught and learned! Yeah! It's our job

**Week 4**
"Capable" means "doing a good job in a timely fashion"

**Week 5**
Post your benchmark results on the back page!
90th Day

**2nd Quarter**

Figure 2.15 Sheet 5 of the miniplanner.

| | | | | | | | | | | | | | | | | | | | | | | Notes |
|---|---|---|---|---|---|---|---|---|---|---|---|---|---|---|---|---|---|---|---|---|---|---|
| **# of Days Left TTT** | x | x | 50 | 49 | 48 | 47 | 46 | 45 | 44 | 43 | 42 | 41 | 40 | 39 | 38 | 37 | 36 | 35 | 34 | 33 | 32 | Week 1 |
| **# of Days Left** | x | x | 89 | 88 | 87 | 86 | 85 | 84 | 83 | 82 | 81 | 80 | 79 | 78 | 77 | 76 | 75 | 74 | 73 | 72 | 71 | |
| | | | M | T | W | Th | F | M | T | W | Th | F | M | T | W | Th | F | M | T | W | Th | F |
| **JANUARY** | | | 21 | 22 | 23 | 24 | 25 | 28 | 29 | 30 | 31 | 1 Feb | 4 | 5 | 6 | 7 | 8 | 11 | 12 | 13 | 14 | 15 |

**Subjects and Times**

WINTER break is over — "No"

STUDENTS

"Change your dance" and they'll change theirs

Let's all write New Year's resolutions and post them.

Teach the "Best thing" not the thing you teach best. Validate the standard.

If a week goes well indicate it. If not, don't repeat it next year!

Talk about Love ♡ They Love it

**Week 2**

"Collective Knowledge" Use it! It empowers all of us!!

MLK DAY

Who was MLK? Share two things.

Remember each time you write a referral it says

PRESIDENTS DAY

**Week 3**

RESPONSIBILITY "Respond with Ability" "We judge ourselves by our intentions but others judge us by our behavior" TTT

#1 You did not connect "Nana's House" and

#2 You can't handle your students In the business world what would happen if you sent your problems to the boss?

HOLIDAY

**Week 4**

We can't get something back unless we give it away.

**Week 5**

Character is what we do or how we act when no one is watching. "Wipe your feet and take your seat" on your own.

FEB
18 19 20 21 22 | 28 67 68 69 70 22

**After School** (Or cut and paste your schedule)

If you were being observed by a secret camera would your behavior get you "Hired or Fired!"

IT MATTERS—Do The Right thing

Progress Reports Go Home

**3rd Quarter**

There is a powerful truth in the left-hand bottom corner of this page. When referrals are written or students are removed from your room, you are sending a message to your boss: I can't handle this situation, this student, this customer, this employee. Think about what would happen if you did that in any other line of work. You would probably lose your job! As a teacher, you at least lose some of your credibility with the principal.

Because of Valentine's Day, February naturally speaks of love. By now you have established an environment of creatively sharing what you love with your students. At times you share your own personal passions or those of your parents or your spouse. Whatever you talk about, make sure your time with your students is also about things that you know about in the real world that make the standards relevant.

## Sheet 6

Sheet 6 brings you to the end of the third marking period, the 135th to the140th day of school (see Figure 2.16). You have never been this far along, ever! A good idea is to have a problem box where students can anonymously communicate their concerns. In the beginning of the year, these problem boxes are usually very full. Post some of these anonymously written problems on the board, and ask the students to start incorporating solutions to solve them. When they do, you will often find that their solutions work far more effectively than something you might have thought of.

## Sheet 7

The seventh page is all about coming back from spring break, a time that was very different this year for all involved (see Figure 2.17). In the next section, I'll explain how you make a deal with your students on the first day of school that you will assign no homework as long as they can show that they really

Figure 2.16 Sheet 6 of the miniplanner.

| | M | T | W | Th | F | M | T | W | Th | F | M | T | W | Th | F | M | T | W | Th | F | M | T | W | Th | F |
|---|---|---|---|---|---|---|---|---|---|---|---|---|---|---|---|---|---|---|---|---|---|---|---|---|---|
| # of Days Left TTT | 27 | 26 | 25 | 24 | 23 | 22 | 21 | 20 | 19 | 18 | 17 | 16 | 15 | 14 | 13 | 12 | 11 | 10 | 9 | X | X | X | X | X | X |
| # of Days Left | 66 | 65 | 64 | 63 | 62 | 61 | 60 | 59 | 58 | 57 | 56 | 55 | 54 | 53 | 52 | 51 | 50 | 49 | 48 | X | X | X | X | X | X |
| FEBRUARY / Mar | 25 | 26 | 27 | 28 | 29 | 3 | 4 | 5 | 6 | 7 | 10 | 11 | 12 | 13 | 14 | 17 | 18 | 19 | 20 | 21 | 24 | 25 | 26 | 27 | 28 |

**Subjects and Times**

MARCH ***** ******** spring break *******

Introduce Presidential Leap Year Trivia

E A R L Y

D I S M I S S A L

Try silent grading on oral reports 1, 2, 3, 4

As you complete the month take down February. Ask "Have you and I applied ourselves totally?"

No one is good at everything. Everyone is good at something. Build Teams

Begin here → Goal is to get here. 135th Day

P.R. means you do things that will send your crew—(customer) home "bragging about the teacher" (coming back for more)

**Left column (Subjects and Times):**

Learn it
Organize it
Validate it
Empower them

Treat students like customers listen to understand not just to reply.

Be Creative! Bring your positive styles to your class. You are the CEO. It's "Your" organization.

**After School (Or cut and paste your schedule):** Think of how you can, not how you can't! If you are not part of the solution, perhaps you are the problem.

**Notes**

Week 1 — Listen to understand—(paraphrase) don't just listen to reply.

Week 2 — Do you know why we have a leap year? You should. As educators we ought to know "Cool Facts"

Week 3 — Use Your Problem Box!!!

Week 4 — Never before accomplished this early

Week 5 — 100% of the standards taught effectively with time to review

Report Cards — Go home on Apr 11

3rd Quarter — Do you see the glass half empty or half full? The choice is yours and theirs

Figure 2.17 Sheet 7 of the miniplanner.

| # of Days Left TTT | 8 | 7 | 6 | 5 | 4 | | 3 | 2 | 1 | | x | 14 | 13 | 12 | 11 | 10 | | | | | | 9 | 8 | 7 | 6 | 5 |
| # of Days Left | 47 | 46 | 45 | 44 | 43 | | 42 | 41 | 40 | 39 | | 38 | 37 | 36 | 35 | 34 | 33 | 32 | 31 | 30 | 29 | 28 | 27 | 26 | 25 | 24 |
| | MARCH 31 | 1 | 2 | 3 | 4 | Apr | 7 | 8 | 9 | 10 | 11 | 14 | 15 | 16 | 17 | 18 | 21 | 22 | 23 | 24 | 25 | 28 | 29 | 30 | 1 | 2 |
| | M | T | W | Th | F | | M | T | W | Th | F | M | T | W | Th | F | M | T | W | Th | F | M | T | W | Th | F |

Begin Review 30

**Notes**

Week 1 — Smart People Review In Nightly Groups

Week 2 — Because Reviewing Everything Affirms Knowledge

Week 3 — We win because of what we know— We lose because of what we don't know!

Week 4 — Average is just as far from the bottom as it is from the top

Week 5 — In the real world—If you are average, you'll not get a raise or a promotion. Make the choice

4th Quarter

**Subjects and Times**

3rd

You'll be done!! They made a deal on day #1 to use this up coming week to review and study

When the state results go into those cume folders they are there FOREVER! So use the time wisely!

The more you Learn The more you EARN $

quarters

TEACHER WORK DAY

EARLY DISMISSAL

Are you behaving like a duck, a chicken, or a robin?

Begin the best review ever!! Read the April chapter and use your glossary effectively

Anything the mind can conceive, or achieve, it can achieve.

MAY — Let them create and give a practice state test

They begin lots of homework now. Remember the deal you made on day 1?

How powerful! Beginning with the end in mind. The deal made on the first day worked!

**After School** (Or cut and paste your schedule)

The very best angle (the best way) to solve a problem is the "TRY Angle"

Progress Reports Go Home

know the standards and as long as they agree to work very hard during this review period leading up to the tests. Standardized tests are just weeks away, so it's time to review, review, review. Note the comment on the upper right-hand corner of the page:

**S**mart **P**eople **R**eview **I**n **N**ightly **G**roups

**B**ecause **R**eviewing **E**verything **A**ffirms **K**nowledge.

Let students create and give a practice test. Turning the state standards into questions is a very effective process for review.

Look at more of what is on this page. For example, "Average is just as far from the bottom as it is from the top." In the very competitive world of business if you were average, you'd be out of business. No one should strive to just be average.

You probably noticed on this page the question, "Are you behaving like a duck, a chicken, or a robin?" All three—the duck, the robin and the chicken—respond differently to storms. (Think of these high-stakes tests as storms that students must endure.)

- The duck allows the water generated by the storm to simply roll off its back. (We can accept what must take place.)

- The chicken gets angry. (We can generate stress by being upset over something we cannot change.)

- That brings us to the robin, which I am told sings during and after a storm. (Or we can look at these difficult tests as being opportunities, rather than obstacles that allow us to become better than we currently are.)

I like to think of the storms in our lives as being lessons, lessons that are gifts that make us stronger and build character. It is our choice how we respond to any given situation. Again, Gandhi says it beautifully, "We must be the change we want to see."

## Sheet 8

The last page of the miniplanner speaks for itself (see Figure 2.18). Testing is the goal. We must remember that if we put our students on task *after* the test, it sends a very confusing message. After the test, do things differently. Take your field trips. Think about scheduling the activity busses the first week of school. That early in the year, most teachers are thinking only about the first week of school. But beginning with the end in mind will help you get there faster, freer, and with a lot more fun than anyone else on the faculty.

With all of your plans now in place, the school year simply flies by, with few issues and lots of joyous teachable moments! That is what the Total Teacher plan accomplishes. It is a brand-new way to energize and excite students, who turn the tide in education from Below Basic to Advanced in just one school year!

Once your plan is complete, you will want to keep it always on your desk or perhaps hung for others to view. Students will want to check to see whether you are on schedule, making them feel very much a part of your plan!

Next we will look at a month-by-month breakdown of so many possibilities that you will want to incorporate into your plan. Remember, it's a work in progress leading to a job well done!

Figure 2.18 Sheet 8 of the miniplanner.

| # of Days Left TTT | | 4 | 3 | 2 | 1 | 0 | | | | | | | | | | | | | | | | | | 3 | 2 | 1 | 0 | | 8 | 7 | 6 | 5 | 4 | | Notes |
|---|---|---|---|---|---|---|---|---|---|---|---|---|---|---|---|---|---|---|---|---|---|---|---|---|---|---|---|---|---|---|---|---|---|---|---|
| # of Days Left | MAY | M 5 | T 6 | W 7 | Th 8 | F 9 | MAY | M 12 | T 13 | W 14 | Th 15 | F 16 | | M 19 | T 20 | W 21 | Th 22 | F 23 | | M 26 | T 27 | W 28 | Th 29 | F 30 | June | M 2 | T 3 | W 4 | Th 5 | F 6 | | |

**Subjects and Times**

Week 1 (MAY 5–9):
You taught it all in a capable fashion and it will come across in their scores!!

Validate the way the cume folder, captures the result of their effort FOREVER!

You finally have the correct tool – The Total Teacher Tool bag and Training

Week 2 / week (MAY 12–23): PACT TESTING

(MAY 26 – June 6): **Trips, Rewards, and have them set up your room for next year**
Now that you got your feet wet and experienced an outstanding year, build on your plans, add improvements & delete what did not work well. Map out your up coming year, then enjoy the summer!

**Notes**

Week 1: The problem is never the problem, it's our attitude about the problem. A+ attitudes win!

Week 2

Week 3

Week 4: Thank you! You are incredible and TOTALLY on your way!

Week 5

4th Quarter

**After School (Or cut and paste your schedule)**

Report Cards Go Home

We are in the business of education. We have a product (knowledge) to sell (transfer). If we sell it correctly (The Total Teacher way) our customers (students) will buy into it. If not, they won't.

— Lorraine

# The Total Teacher Year

*Month-by-Month Tips for Making the Most
of Your School Year*

Thousands of teachers find themselves in the same predicament year after year: sitting out the summer, wondering how their dream of becoming a teacher turned into a nightmare. By now, after reading the previous sections, you know that the coming year is going to be totally different, totally great, and totally transformed. For the first time, you understand many things and feel that you are finally in control. It's June and you've read the book, you understand the logic, and you've filled out your planner. Now it's time to look into the future, month by month, to look at some other things you can do as a Total Teacher, and to get a glimpse of just how different things will be. We begin this chapter in June and July simply because, in a traditional calendar, teachers are usually off during these two months and so have time to plan the next year, but it doesn't matter when you decide to plan and implement the process. Whether you start in June, July, January, or April, you will now have a guide to do it your way, on your own timetable, suit your plan perfectly for your grade level, your cultural and creative needs, and your own holidays, ideas, school events, or calendar breaks. Your calendar can also be broken down into quarters, into semesters, into A-B fashion, or into forty-five-day miniclass cycles. It is an outline that can be used in every possible setting.

# June and July

*J*une and July will be true vacations from now on. In future years, once the school year is over, and you have your placement for the next year, as well as your school calendar for the upcoming year, you will probably only have to take out your markers and stickers (or your computer) and the standards, and simply tweak what you already have in place.

Everything from the previous year will be fresh in your mind as you revise and think about new relevant ways to teach the standards. You can use the back page of your planner to indicate your students' test scores from last year and compare them to this year's, validating your AYP (annual yearly progress). You'll smile with pride as you notice how many students who began at Below Basic have moved to Basic or even Proficient and Advanced while they were in your class. Some teachers also keep a narrative on that page so that there is a month-by-month reminder of what took place. The end-of-grade test scores will no longer be stashed somewhere, hardly accessible; they will be right in your planner. July truly gives you one full month totally off with no worries. Your plan is in place!

# August

Summer was especially restful, and now it is time to get to work, and you are more than eager to begin! But before the students arrive, you should give some thought to the surroundings. What kind of physical experience do you want yourself and your students to have in your classroom—your place of business? Like your own home, your classroom can have a welcoming fragrance and a welcome mat by the door. You can decorate with posters you designed yourself with your favorite sayings and with balloons with happy faces. Your own corner of the classroom can be arranged to look like the executive space of a well organized leader. An inexpensive executive chair and framed diplomas and awards can remind you and others that you are well educated, well trained, and certified to do your job in an outstanding fashion. Make your classroom an empowering, inviting, and engaging place to spend the next 180 days!

Classroom management will be much easier this year as well. One technique is to number each desk by placing a small sticker in the corner. Then have duplicate numbers on pieces of paper in a jar. On Fridays have each student pick a number out of the jar and move their things to their new location for one week. It's a very simple strategy that students truly enjoy. And it's more than just an enjoyable practice because, if a student's grade point average should happen to drop for any reason, suspending this seat rotation until it once again increases is extremely effective.

Before the first day of class, make a sample sheet that shows the countdown so that students can internalize how you will be counting backward to your goal of learning the standards in 140 days. They will be able to see and understand the countdown and how it will make things obviously different. Both your miniplanner and working planner have the following countdown conveniently placed at the top of each page, keeping you on task academically and teaching creatively

| | | | | | |
|---|---|---|---|---|---|
| Number of days to learn | 140 | 139 | 138 | 137 | 136 |
| Number of days in attendance | 179 | 178 | 177 | 176 | 175 |
| August | M-20 | T-21 | W-23 | Th-24 | F-25 |

Every year I begin my teaching year, as any good business meeting begins, by setting a positive tone—and a very different tone from that of the other teachers. I truly believe that the way something begins is indicative of how it will end. I also believe that no one gets a second chance at a first impression. On that first day of school, I am especially cognizant of sending positive, productive, and inspiring messages that convey two things: (1) I really care about and enjoy my students. (2) I truly love my chosen profession of teaching!

I do something that I think is important only because I have never attended a business meeting in the corporate world without this characteristic. I want to set the tone of being the CEO of a competitive, upbeat, profitable business, and I want to send the message that the students are my employees. As I greet the students and ask them to take seats, they quickly notice a small, attractive buffet-type table set up at the back of the room.

On that table are some minidonuts or brownies, hard candy, small drinks, and fruit. This is probably the best spent "business expense" any teacher could incur. It is a very inexpensive way to make a lasting impression on the first day of a life-changing experience: a very different school year. I am all about making memories. If we don't celebrate the special, wonderful days and events, they tend to escape us. The first day of a new school year certainly warrants some somewhat of a celebratory difference. So even if it is only juice, donuts, and a pretty table, it sends a message that says I care about you, I think you are special, and today is a very important day!

The students are invited to fix a small plate, grab a napkin, and bring their snacks back to their seats. It is important for them to get comfortable before I begin because what I have to say is important, and a message that will be very new toall of them. I will share some of what I say to my sixth-grade students; however, the same message can be geared up to high school or geared down to first grade. Teachers can quickly see how this can be delivered with a middle school spin by simply changing the examples, which will be yours anyway. I am speaking to sixth-graders in this section, but this introduction can be altered in a way that excites high school students, alternative school participants, even adult learners who are attending graduate classes, as you can see in my DVDs.

> Ladies and gentlemen, hello. My name is Mrs. Milark and I am very glad to have you here. What I have to say is extremely important and very different from anything that you've heard on the first day of school in the past. I'd like you to get comfortable, and be prepared to sit for a little longer than usual. If anyone needs to use the restroom before we begin, please do so now. I really do not want to be interrupted.

As I begin, I let them know that in no uncertain terms this is *my place of business* and that later today they will have applications to fill out and resumes to prepare. For now, I need their attention so that I can let them know how different the next 180 days will be.

> I want to welcome you to a very different school year, unlike any you have had in the past. I am going to ask you to listen to me with an open mind, because at the end of my orientation, you will have to make a choice. Life is all about learning. The more you learn, the more you earn, and life is all about learning lots of things so that you can earn wonderful experiences in all that life has to offer. The way to power is through knowledge. Unfortunately, we have only one hundred and eighty days to spend together in order to accomplish our mission. Our goal is to get promoted to the next grade. It's like that in the world of business as well. People work hard so that they can go on to the next level. Their work ethic usually earns them a promotion. When your behavior and attitude complement your ability, there is no stopping success!
>
> In this class, we will operate with pretty much the same mind-set. The tests that you will take at the end of the year determine how well you have learned things and how well you remember and apply that knowledge. Those tests take place about ten days before school is over. You can look on that wall and see the calendars that indicate just that. I have already clearly marked the days we will be sending wonderful results to the state department. Those tests will prove to the superintendent of education that this is the smartest class that has ever come down the pike. Your rate of improvement will be greater than any they have ever seen. That's because this year you will be better prepared than ever before. You will also enjoy the next one hundred and eighty days more than any other school year you have ever engaged in.
>
> Let me tell you why. [*I hold up my yearlong planner or projected it onto the smart board from my PC so that they can see that I have filled it out for the entire year.*] I spent the entire summer laying out our school year, and I will pass out this week's countdown and assignment sheet a little later today.

You see, I have a plan that is like a road map that will keep us on the right track at all times. It will help us make sure that you not only know but understand all the state standards that you will be tested on. In about one hundred and forty days, you will have learned everything there is to learn for the year, and you will all take part in very thorough review.

First and foremost, there will be little to *no homework!* [*This is a real attention getter!*] No homework for anyone who truly learns the lesson in class, and I will check for understanding daily, so not only I but you will know whether you really know the material or not! If you haven't mastered a standard or lesson, then you will have homework. The reason is simple. We will have one class rule, and that is:

*Effective communication is always kind, gentle, and respectful, therefore fair!*

Always, no exceptions! You are probably asking yourself, so what does that have to do with homework? Well, it is very simple. If you don't apply yourself and don't take your job of the day seriously, letting a standard or lesson go unmastered, you do two things: One, you bring our class GPA down. GPA stands for grade point average, something we calculate almost daily and post on our curves. Second, you also hold up the rest of the class. That is neither *kind*, nor *gentle* and certainly not *respectful* or fair of everyone else's time.

It is perfectly all right to make mistakes in this class, which is how we learn. We all learn from our mistakes, and we will occasionally share how those mistakes happened. I am adamant about learning from our mistakes. That is why there are erasers on pencils. However, I am also adamant about not repeating a mistake. It's all right to make mistakes, but it is *not* all right *not* to learn from the mistakes we make: that is how we stop making them.

I want this to be a safe, comfortable place for all of us. You are all too big to have an adult monitoring your every move. Character is what someone does when no one else is looking. Let me pose a few questions to you.

They are rhetorical, so please do not respond to them, simply process them in your own mind.

- Do you want your mom or dad to dress you?
- Do you want your mom or dad to feed you or pick out your food when you go out to eat?
- Do you need your mom or dad to pick out your clothes or give you a bath?

I don't think so. Will your mom or dad be taking your final exam for you? I don't think so. Well, with that said, it is not your mom or dad's job to clean out and organize your backpack or to remind you to do an assignment or even to be the threat that keeps your behavior in check. All of the things I just mentioned are choices that you make by yourself, for yourself to improve yourself. If a bad choice is made from time to time, then you can rectify the bad choice with an apology and take the opportunity to not make a bad choice in that area again.

Let's move on. I am on your team. I am your best advocate. I will go to your defense. I am the best ally you have: Don't test me, don't cross me, and most of all remember you do not want to get on the wrong side of me. That means the following: Do not lie, do not be disrespectful, and, most of all, don't give me any surprises. I don't like surprises. I won't throw surprises at you, and I don't expect them tossed at me. You will know what is coming, you will know what is expected, and I want to make you a promise right now: I will never give you busywork. There is simply no time to waste on that. I am responsible for bringing out all your hidden positive and productive potential, and I have a gut feeling that you guys are brilliant!

On the wall there is a full complement of calendars. Calendars are the fundamental motivators for most business. Let's look at these calendars. Do you see this "one seventy-nine" next to today's date? That is telling us that we have only one hundred and seventy-nine more chances to interact. Do you see the "one hundred forty" right above the "one seventy-nine"? That "one hundred forty" means that I have to be done teaching you all the state standards in one hundred and forty days (and, as you can see, that will be right around spring break) so that we have plenty of time to review before finals. I also will assign little or no homework until right here in the third quarter, at which time you will have a great deal of homework, but it will be homework that will enable you to ace your finals.

Ladies and gentlemen, the way that we manage to have almost no homework is to go into an agreement right here and now. The agreement is this. I will present you with the best possible instruction during class. I will teach you to the best of my ability. I will pass out the state standards in thirds and help you understand each and every one. I take my job very seriously. I love what I do and will do it every day to the best of my ability for you. I will continually use your ideas and keep your interest level pegged and your educational level increasing. We will engage in current topics as well as in interesting discussions to make the standards relevant to your world.

In return, *you* need to work unbelievably hard while in my room. I mean harder than you've ever worked before because the benefits will be greater than you've ever had before. You will learn how to take notes and how to use highlighters and retain most if not all of what I teach. If you don't grasp a concept, it will be your responsibility to get together with a classmate who has mastered it. Our class information, such as the results of previous tests, will be posted at all times on these curves, as will our (ever increasing) grade point average. You will personally be aware of knowing how to master a standard. You can ask yourself whether you can teach a particular standard to someone else and whether you understand how to transfer it to your own world. You will also be able to assess yourself by understanding that you have really mastered a particular standard when you are able to apply it to the real world. These simple internalizations will allow you to better prepare yourself before you prove your knowledge by taking a test, and then continue to track your own improvements. This creates a real team effort.

One more thing: These are my rules and they can change. If for one minute you feel you want to cut up, be slack, not apply yourself to giving me all you are capable of giving me, we can revert to the traditional techniques of the classrooms you have been part of in the past: no treats, no calendars, no countdowns, lots of rules rather than one rule, lots of homework all year, rather than little to no homework until spring break. *This is your choice.* I am very capable of teaching you either way. Of course, what I've outlined is my preferred method, but this is a team and it has to be a mutual agreement.

Before we make a decision, I want to talk to you about your cumulative folders. Every year your picture is taken and placed in these very important folders. Then, all that takes place all year, how many days you are tardy, how many days you are absent, any personal milestones, such as your parents being deployed, or if they were divorced this year, or if you earned some sort of an award—it all goes into the cumulative folder. If you move, it follows you; when you apply for a job and your employer wants to know about your academic ability, it is all there. Plus it's your ticket for a free college education. Scholarships are available to students who truly apply themselves prior to graduation, and it's all right here in these folders. I have no doubt that this year we will enter test scores that will rock the system with major improvements. I can feel it; you are truly a great class. Look at how you are behaving this morning. Each of you is incredibly attentive, you are making eye contact, nodding your head when you understand and exhibiting body language that makes me think you are four or five years older than you actually are. Let me tell you, I am impressed!

You know I am really very interested in learning all I can about you. So let me put our first choice on our calendars. I am going to go to next Monday and write "BIO." This is *not* an assignment because you don't have to do it. I would really like the opportunity to know as much about you as you want me to know. So I will give anyone who turns in his or her biography 100 points as sort of a cushion to counteract any fumbles you may have later. You will not be penalized for not doing it, but will benefit numerically if you chose to do it.

I usually stop here and say, "Let's shift gears and learn a little bit about each other." I then tell them about myself, my children, my husband, my life prior to teaching, my time living on a boat with my husband, and some of my favorite stories. I also ask that each of them introduce themselves by using this fun icebreaker. This really helps me remember their names.

I am now going to go around the room, and I want you to tell me your name and then a favorite food that begins with the same letter. I would say my name is Lorraine and I love lettuce. My husband's name is Bill, and he loves broccoli. You get the idea. Let's go around the room one time, and then I will get back to the business at hand. Please stand up when it is your turn.

This is a great way for you to make a mental note of all those names that you want to learn as quickly as possible.

Ladies and gentlemen, now that we have had the opportunity to stretch and have heard from everyone, let me reiterate where I am coming from. I very much believe in the word "responsibility." As you can see, the last part of that word is "ability." Most people have a philosophy or a belief about life. Well, that word will be the very foundation of this class. You must take full responsibility for yourself, for your choices, and for your actions, simply because it is your life, and the blame game is neither kind, nor gentle, nor respectful. When you respond with ability, you leave a positive impression. I see you as well educated young adults, and I must say I am already impressed.

They need the kudos! After an hour or so of chatting with them, a tone is established that they want to continue.

I want to drive home the point of being responsible. If your mom or dad or whoever does the grocery shopping decided not to shop because they didn't want to, you'd be pretty upset. What if the cafeteria staff decided that they did not want to make lunch today? Wow, I think we'd all be rather angry. Or if the custodians stopped taking out the trash or cleaning the restrooms. Each time they shunned their responsibility, they would make us unhappy. Well, the effect is the same when you are not responsible, when you chose to not do something because it is either difficult or you simply don't feel like it: Not living up to your responsibility usually angers many people. The bottom line is this: We all must realize that we have a responsibility to do the things that are required of us, no matter how much we may not want to. It is part of being grown up.

During this introductory chat, I am very conscious of *not* sounding like Mr. Rogers. If we talk down to students rather than treating them like the young adults that they are, then we lose them right off the bat. High expectations give you higher-than-expected results. Treat them as you want them to act. Remember, they hate being bored or babied.

Everyone who has ever been a student of mine, in elementary school, middle school, high school or even the graduate classes that I teach, has heard a few bicycle stories and here is one for you.

I would like you all to think about the first time you took off, zooming away without training wheels. Most of us go on for a long time before the training wheels come off, still not able to master the balancing act that a two-wheeler demands. Often many days go by with our moms or dads running behind us, saying something like, "Pedal and steer and balance, pedal and steer and balance." They become totally exhausted, running alongside you, holding onto the bicycle seat and trying to keep you from falling off. Falling at this crucial time when you are learning could be disastrous, so they keep running. I remember doing this with all four of our children, and getting totally exhausted and exasperated! They laugh. [*What better sound than children's laughter? There is none!*]

The point is this: Ladies and gentlemen, suddenly there is what we call an epiphany moment! That is a wonderful vocabulary word, and I want you to use that word often. It means to have a sudden realization, a sudden intuitive leap of understanding, especially one that comes through an ordinary but striking occurrence. It's a very dramatic turning point. It's like suddenly having the aha light go on when you are figuring out a difficult math problem. Here is the point: Until *you* are ready, until *you* decide to ride that bike or look at that word problem from a different point of view, it is not going to happen. This is very, very important, and I will say it again: Until *you* are ready and *you* decide *you want to* master that problem or master riding that bike, it is not going to happen! That is the same way it works with schoolwork. Once you decide you are going to master a particular lesson you will! "Anything the mind can conceive and believe it can achieve" is a very true statement. You can go through all the motions, but unless you want it to happen, it is just not going to happen. I can run behind you, just like your moms did and say something like, "Study and read and remember, study and read and remember." [*Here I pretend to be running behind a bicycle holding on to a seat, slightly bent over and repeating the words, "Study and read and remember" over and over to make my point!*]

It is my job to present you with all the knowledge possible. It's my job to show you ways to remember it all. But it is your job to take it from there. How many of you think you are capable of doing that? . . .

Good, great!

At this time I will hand you what college students call a "syllabus." It is a list of the standards that you will be responsible for by the forty-fifth day of school. It is also an outline that has two numbers on it, plus a countdown that supports the numbers on our calendars. Those two countdowns begin with one hundred seventy-nine. That indicates that, as of today, you will have to get up and get here one hundred seventy-nine more times. The other number is one hundred thirty-nine, which means that in one hundred thirty-nine more days, you would have learned all the standards, one-third at a time, and we will then begin counting the number of days to the final state exam. That will give us about eight to nine weeks to go over all the material yet another time. That is when we will agree to really have tons of homework because, remember, those state scores go into your permanent files.

I want all of you to memorize the words on this poster. What it says is very important.

No one is good at everything,

But everyone is good at something.

This entire year will be a team effort, and we are all on the same team, so if in the past there were cliques or groups that did not interact well with each other, that will simply not be the case for the remaining one hundred seventy-nine days. From this point on we are family: helping, not hindering; appreciating, not aggravating each other. Is this understood? . . .

Great. Let's move on.

There will always be neighbors we love and others, well—let's just say they are not the ones we choose to invite over for a barbecue.

In a neighborhood, in a community, and in a classroom, we all need to learn how to get along. Ladies and gentlemen, I am adamant about this class being run like a family, like a winning team. You are all on my team, and the underlying motto is to be in all things kind, gentle, and respectful! This is how things will work in here. Will I assign seats? No. Will you pick our own seats? No. OK, then how will it work? Every desk has a number on it. If you look really closely, the numbers are very inconspicuously placed on the front right-hand corner of each desk. [*This is something you take care of during those two weeks before the students arrive.*] Can everyone see the numbers on your desks? In this jar I am holding, there are corresponding numbers. This way of choosing your seats represents probability in action. We will master a math objective while changing seats. I told you this class would be fun! Every Friday, you will pick a number, then move to your new place, next to a new person, with whom you will learn and maximize your potential.

Let me share a story that really happened. One year when I was teaching on the Marine Corps Air Station—a really nice place to work, with lots of cool jets everywhere—I had two people who were not very good friends in my class. We picked new seats every Friday afternoon. There are only thirty-seven Fridays in the entire school year. The first few Fridays went by and occasionally someone would end up sitting next to the same person as during a previous week. Well, these two young men were obviously meant to be friends, or perhaps learn from each other, because out of thirty-seven picks, they picked each other twenty-two times! We kept track and so will you. In the back of your flash card box, there will be one card with everyone's name on it, where you will keep a tally of how often you sit next to a particular person. Doing this, we can better understand probability—a math standard that most people learn but rarely master.

There is one more part to this seat rotation. I am now going to pass out a manila envelope with your name on it. Inside there is a blank piece of paper. Each week, just before you pick your new seat numbers, you will get the folder of the person you are sitting next to. You then will write two new wonderful things you discover about that person. Two positive comments that compliment something about the person and that perhaps you never took the time or had the opportunity to notice prior to sitting with them and working with them for a full week. At the end of thirty-seven weeks, each of you will have about seventy-four new insights to yourself, written by your classmates. You will have new things, nice things that other people noticed about you. Again, it is about choice, you can choose to see the annoying things about others or choose to hone in on their really wonderful attributes.

Perhaps now is a good time to look at the poster with the glass on it and to see whether you can understand the meaning of viewing something as being either half full or half empty. It is all about your perception being positive or negative.

There are more exemplary outcomes to this procedure than you can imagine, and my students especially like working this way. When we talk about paired studying later, you will see the enormous benefits of this subliminal way of enforcing team interaction.

Very little works if it does not have the elements of give-and-take. A win/win situation must be created. That is what you have just created, and students want to take advantage of your deal! Little ever gets accomplished without enthusiasm, desire, and transference of a shared goal. Realizing their world is far more instantaneous than ours was, we must embrace their times and their needs rather than fight them. Give the class instantaneous and continuous goals, along with support and encouragement, so that they can achieve them, because they want to, and you will have a winning scenario on your hands!

In just a couple of hours you have generated a new sought-after energy—a new mind-set—and your students are thrilled, able, and ready! They want to accept the academic challenges you outlined for them. Your direction is now their direction. You will get more work out of this class than any time a teacher stands up in front of the room and dumbs them down, talking to them as if they were little children unable to think any faster than molasses flows in January. If you give them boring mediocrity, then you will get boring mediocrity. Give them enthusiasm and energy and part of yourself, and you will get those things in return. If you keep doing what you are doing, you will keep getting what you are getting. So leave that slow, boring, condescending talk to others. It does not belong in a classroom where we expect students to aggressively attack those state standards.

Before concluding this segment, always check for understanding by giving them a four question quiz, each question worth 25 points, then plotting the outcome on the Curve. Those who got all four question correct obviously retained the information and are advanced. Those who only managed to get one question correct retained none of what was taught, are below basic for today, and will therefore have homework. Make sure that you leave a few minutes at the end of each lesson to ask, "Are there any questions or comments?" Then take the necessary time to answer their questions, thanking them for indulging you as well.

This is a great time to give the students a fun project. Have each student cut strips of paper of equal length that will be looped together with staples. You will need 180 total strips. Now link the strips together to create a chain that can be strung across your room. At the end of each day, have a student remove a link by some process you establish, such as in alphabetical order, or perhaps a girl-boy rotation, maybe even choosing the person who had the roughest day, allowing that person to reach a little higher tomorrow. Little by little the first forty-five links will disappear by the time the first report card goes home. By Thanksgiving, almost half of the chain will no longer be visible, and students will quickly have a tangible reminder that they are mastering all those standards that used to slip away from them in the past.

Before ending the first day of school, you can do one more powerful thing. Pass out some large, unlined paper, and ask everyone to draw a picture of his or her family, labeling everyone they choose to include. On the back, let them tell you about their world and their families, using any format they choose. This exercise sends a profound message, a very special message that they hear as, "This teacher cares! This teacher really wants to know about me and my world. I am not just a body filling a chair." This simple exercise also provides a wealth of information.

The first day is over. What a success! Everyone is excited. The students leave. You just know it is going to be the best year ever, and you think to yourself, "Gosh I really enjoyed today!" As you leave with their drawings, you are eager to look into and vicariously visit some of the families shown in your students' meaningful artwork. Perhaps you will better understand what they are all going home to this evening. Perhaps some issues that they have to deal with will become obvious to you through their drawings, giving you a compassionate spin on them as people. It will allow you to get just a little deeper into their lives, giving you a better understanding of these very special wonderful people whom you just met today.

Before August is over, you should have

- Pretested everyone.

- Talked about the standards that they know but may have forgotten over the summer.

- Walked everyone through the first third of the standards to model how much they already know.

August will soon be over, and both you and the students will be aware of how quickly it disappeared! The first month, although short, will be a smashing success! You will feel the emergence of self-esteem and positive thinking. Their questions and comments will elevate the bar daily. The students will know that you truly believe that their questions (provided they respond with ability) are worthy. They will love having a list of the standards. It will feel great to highlight the ones they have mastered.

Students keep all the work they do for the first forty-five days, and then it goes into an envelope or folder to be handed back and used as part of their review in the spring. I especially enjoy using FedEx envelopes. They hold everything nicely and are a constant reminder of seeing what most people do not see: that arrow between the *E* and the *X*. Everything that is turned in is folded in half, with the name, date, and subject on the upper right and side of a folded paper. The grade is posted inside for confidentiality, never with the number of *wrong* answers, but always with the number of items that are *correct*! For example, if the answer column had ten possible answers and the student managed to answer eight correctly, the mark would be "8/10."

Shifting gears frequently makes learning fun, and it allows you to tell real stories, applying the lessons to real life. The average attention span is not more than twenty minutes, so make sure you maximize each and every minute with lots of transitions, keeping their attention like a great movie that has them on the edge of their seats.

There will be a great deal of self-monitoring by the students. You just can't go too fast for them—they really do keep up. Go too slowly, however, and you lose them in a heartbeat! Students go home raving about the best teacher and class they ever had. Parents will be amazed at how much their children talk about school and don't want to miss any days under any circumstance. The really amazing part is parents will come and tell you how responsible their children have become! It feels so good when you simply smile and give those parents a quick wink that says, "You have a wonderful child!"

August is the time to review much of what they have already learned in previous grades. Show them how to make flash cards and point out how to find various standards explained in their textbooks and online. Respect the fact that the class has a multitude of retention levels and allow students to pair up and help each other. You will be surprised at how well they apply themselves. The teamwork begins here; relish the interaction and the positive brainstorming that they engage in because they truly know that they have a united goal, with an understanding mentor. It is not an us-versus-them attitude any longer. Now *we* have a job to do, and *we* will get it done together and show the world our accomplishments. We will blow test scores out of the water and be fine examples for all who are observing.

The month flies by, and everyone proudly accomplishes the goals set for all subjects in all areas with time left over to do other things. You've been able to go outdoors and look at the clouds, and the students write papers describing the taste of the candy they were eating, using more adjectives than ever imagined in the past. What a way to teach!

At the end of August, fill out this checklist for yourself:

☐ Are you and the students all on time and on task?

☐ Are all the standards being looked at, talked about, and covered daily?

☐ Did you stay upbeat and move along as scheduled?

☐ Do the students still enjoy using their new tools, such as TTTA, Curves, Calendars, Countdowns, and all the new things you've introduced?

☐ Are they taking notes?

☐ Are you letting them know how pleased you are with their performance?

☐ Are they able to tell you what standards they have truly mastered?

☐ Did you make a big deal of covering up the month of August on your calendar wall with all the standards that have been mastered?

☐ Do they understand that August of this year will never ever be captured again and that, if they did not use each and every day to the max, they lost out?

☐ Did you ask the question that truly matters at the end of the month: "Have you been as productive as possible?"

☐ Did each student do at least one drawing for you?

☐ Did you change seats using the lottery method every Friday?

☐ Did they write positive comments about those they sat next to?

☐ Do you prompt students to go home and rave, rather than rant, about school?

☐ Have you diligently removed the links from your chain and crossed off days on the calendars. Remember that students are visual!

☐ Turn in a narrative to your principal that proves all that you have accomplished. Eventually administration will realize that an actual narrative of what has taken place far exceeds those plans that are all about what teachers attempt to get done!

Staying on task is not magic. You just have to chip away at it. Jot down the little things that you do and insert them into your plan to be used next year, increasing your own productive potential. You are creating a wonderful system, a system that will breed success for you and for everyone you teach. It is going to be one heck of a dinner party; the mood is set, by the time everyone indulges in dessert (final exams) you will be asked for the recipe! You have sent the message that matters: "I will give you what you want, and, in return, I believe you will accept what I know you need."

This is what I use. It works for me, but you can create your own personalized version. Remember that all I am doing is letting you know how I begin my first day of classes. You will see the very negative attitude of the students transform right before your eyes, beginning with the first day of school.

Research shows that two consecutive years of condescending negativity in a classroom can do irreparable damage to children. We need to try to change those statistics. We really have no control over what children must endure at the hands of their parents, but we can make sure that school is a very safe place for them to learn, to experience, and to enjoy being exposed to positive, productive situations that enable them to make good choices. Let me share an old Chinese proverb that says it all:

A child's life is like a piece of paper on which every passerby leaves a mark.

# September

*L*abor Day weekend has been thoroughly enjoyable, and the real work on standards, school, and success now begins. The class is excited, and you are far better prepared than ever. You are no longer being approached by each day. Rather, you are now approaching each day with a definitive plan, a primary aim, which is well thought-out and in place but that still leaves lots of room for spontaneity, creativity, and flexibility. You smile when you look at your Total Teacher Planner and are amazed at all the things that you are able to capture so easily. It all fits together so nicely, with lots of time to spare. Imagine that! Don't you love it? You write no referrals, and your classroom management skills are enviable! Your strategies are the topic of everyone's conversation in the teacher's lounge.

For about $2, you can put a candy kiss on everyone's desk one day in September to say, "I am so glad you are here." If you have the time, put a simple index card under that little piece of candy with a personally written note. You had no homework to deal with, and this little note will take very little time and will be far more effective than any assignment. Tell them something that makes them feel special. The return on this investment is miraculous!

The first day after Labor Day can be celebrated and referred to in your planner with pride. If approached in this manner with these four incredibly simple tools—the Curves, the Clocks, the Calendars, and the Countdowns—the class will embrace laboring. Share freely and often the fact that you have planned out the entire year and that you all have a scheduled goal that you must get to together. If the plan is executed correctly, everyone will have many hours to do things of choice, such as read great books, play sports, and learn a new hobby.

At this time you may want to share that we often judge others by their behavior and judge ourselves by our intentions. This will further unite the class. They certainly expect me to do my job professionally (my intentions ought to match my behavior). They expect the same level of excellence from their dentist, their doctor, or their cafeteria staff. What is good for one should be good for all! Once this point is brought to their attention, applied in a way they enjoy, there is literally no stopping them or the team they are on. Model a commendable work ethic and then let them emulate it.

*Effort is directly linked to the expectation of success!*

With these discussions, students begin to internalize why they need to accept full responsibility for doing their jobs. They now have a personal and very doable expectation of their own success, and that really drives everyone to a new level of positive and productive self motivating achievement.

An enjoyable way to complete this concept is to give them each a manila folder and let them personalize it in any way they want to. Explain that throughout the next 45 days every time they create something academic and standards based—something they are proud of—they can slide it into this folder. Each marking period, they will get a new folder, and then when it is time to review they will have a collection of their best work. They must keep a tally of what goes into the folder. This tally will show them that concepts that may have been difficult to begin with have been mastered.

September begins incredibly well. It is a unique time. Your main objective is to stay focused on your time line and on your Total Teacher Plan. Realize that though you may fall behind or move forward, not always working exactly as planned; that is perfectly fine. Things happen, and going with the flow is normal. In about two more weeks you will be sending home progress or interim reports; then about three weeks later, report cards go home. The class enjoys learning about the business concepts, each day gaining more and more of a perspective on time: hourly (with Clocks) daily (with Curves) monthly (with Calendars) and annually (with Countdowns). You'll be covering all of the material that you know must be covered with a deep-seated feeling that everyone in the room really wants to move to the right side of the curve as quickly and as effectively as possible.

Help the class with little ways to remember what is being taught. Teach them how to transcribe facts from their notebooks onto flash cards that they can take with them anywhere to help them study. Self-made flash cards are very effective. Check periodically to make sure that they are creating and using them. Let students know that there will be frequent four-question quizzes, with each question being worth 25 points, to help them identify whether they are Below Basic, Basic, Proficient, or Advanced on any given standard. Plot the results on a curve: One correct = 25 points, but still at the Below Basic end of the curve. Two correct = 50 points, moving them to a Basic position. Three correct = 75 points, pushing them over the hump to a Proficient place on the curve. When they can answer all four correctly, they earn 100 points and are proudly at the Advanced position, empowering them with the ability to help others. These quizzes will be point-producing, not penalizing, allowing the students to feel successful, and having tangible proof that they are making progress (moving from the left to the right side of the curve). Make the lessons energetic, full of relevant trivia, and informative.

Fridays seem to show up really quickly. This is the day when everyone reaches into a bucket, pulls out a new seat number, and moves to a new location. Prior to doing that, they must fill out the folder with the person's name on it that they just spent five days sitting next to. They learned a great deal about this new friend because your new format allowed them to work together sharing their strengths with each other. They now become evaluators and enter two positive sentences about something they discovered about that person. They eagerly change seats once again, with desks being cleaned out and organized, moving on to the next week with a new air of excitement: Students embrace change that they know empowers them!

During the last three weeks of September, you will be covering material you entered into your plan way back in June. Your planner keeps you right on schedule in many different areas, and next year will be even better, if you can imagine that. There is enough extra time to read one of your favorite short books out loud. Work is being accomplished at a pace you only dreamed about in years past.

September is often full of unpredictable weather. Use those days to your advantage by noting that weather moves from West to East, and point out the position of the flag on a windy day to show them where the wind is blowing from. When there is a huge temperature change, or wind shift, these lessons become interesting and memorable. Later on, look at your planner, find where these lessons were supposed to be taught and indicate that they have already been mastered on the days that provided actual examples. What a delightful way to keep things organized. The days that were set aside for teaching weather can now be used for other things, because when the conditions are right, everyone masters things more quickly, leaving lots more free time!

The last week of September means that the first several weeks of school are over. The Countdown should be posted and referred to often. It is on the Calendars and changed daily on the board, and these updates help everyone get far more punctual. This will become fun. It does not mean your classroom or lessons will be rowdy or unorganized. It does mean things will no longer be monotonous and boring.

Progress reports go home the last week of the month. A very nice (and well received) touch is allowing students to design their own form that allows them to indicate the progress that they feel they are making in each area of instruction as well as their goal for the remainder of the quarter. I feel strongly that the students must share in the writing and illustrating of the progress report because the student needs to make the progress, set the goal, and then achieve that goal. The progress report should not be an "I gotcha" report from the teacher that snags the students and points out their shortcomings. It ought to be an indicator that they are responsible and that they are responding to areas where they plan to do better because they want to and know they can!

The completed progress report gets turned in to you, and you can add your comments to each area. Parents enjoy reading these special reports from their children and often ask to keep them rather than signing and returning them. This type of report is far more personal because it is from their now very responsible, child! Often the students want to make the report into a booklet with a page for each subject, being very thorough and descriptive. Some students make it into a graph, and others just write lengthy statements.

Another strategy to introduce in September is a concept I call "Dig It." It works like this. I tell them what we will be covering in the next class. They then are asked to go home and *dig into it*—learning all they can on their own by reading the material I assign them. During the next class, they will get a four-question quiz. If they get every question correct, then they know that they know it, and they will have no studying to do at home unless they *want* to. By now they realize that not "digging it" is not kind, gentle, or respectful. They understand that it is not fair to delay the class schedule because someone did not "get it" due to his or her lack of application at home on standards that were difficult; homework becomes a choice. Of course, they have to sit through the lesson, but they will be exempt from homework because they proved that they have already mastered the key concepts. In essence, they are studying so that they don't have to study. They are learning more because they are finding things out by themselves and because they want to instead of your feeding them and forcing them to retain information. This is a teacher's dream: You are creating a classroom full of lifelong learners.

At the end of September, take a moment and assess your own progress:

☐ Are you where your timetable indicates you ought to be? If you are a bit ahead, great! Keep going. If you are behind, don't panic, make adjustments, consolidate, and teach from experience, not the text, in order to get caught up!

☐ Have a flash card check to make sure your students are creating and using their flash cards. A simple "Wow, that looks great" or "I like those colored cards" becomes a constructive and caring comment!

☐ Have you kept everyone abreast of how many days are left until the end of the year?

☐ Did you cross off the days all month, and cover the Calendar with all the standards that have been mastered? Give yourself and your students a huge Ta Da! moment when you look at the Calendar at the end of the month!

☐ Did you have your students change seats?

☐ Have you validated their mature manners with compliments?

☐ Have you shared at least one or two personal stories to support any particular standard?

☐ Is the class really moving along? If it is, the students will say things like, "Wow, is it time to go home already?" or "I really like school this year."

☐ Ask yourself, "Am I having lots more fun these days?" The answer ought to be a great big *yes*!

# October

*H*alloween can be scary, but not this year because you've been using the Total Teacher Plan and are on time teaching all the standards. Report cards go out at the end of the month in most school districts, and you find yourself wondering how you ever functioned without this type of a plan. Thinking and acting like a Total Teacher really fits perfectly into who you are. It also enhances who the students are and who they can become! You really seem to be enjoying this class so much more than any other class you ever had. There are virtually no discipline problems, parents and principals are happy, and everyone is involved with each other in a positive way. It seems as if you are teaching adults; the class enjoys learning, the discussions are great, and they seem to be peppered with new vocabulary words.

Introducing current events is the highlight of October. As the students become more aware, their world erupts with new and interesting things that have always been there but that are now noticed far more frequently. Take a few moments to explain that being informed is one of the fundamental criteria of being well educated. That alone makes them sit up taller and display a sense of pride; they are more educated, and it feels great! Set aside some time each day or each week to discuss current events. Things like elections, natural disasters, and even sporting events can be tied into standards in language arts, math, science, or social studies. When you use current, relevant incidents to teach the standards, the subject matter becomes interesting and in the now.

Here's one way to approach current events. Divide the number of students in your class by five, then assign each group a day of the week (or month depending on how often you want to do this). For example, the first six people in the class will have Monday. Give them a week to prepare a report to the class. They need to pick a news item, take notes answering who, what, when, where, and why they chose that story. On Monday, the six students will report on their topic, with each student speaking for just two to three minutes. And after the report, the whole class will discuss the event. Initially their presentations probably will not be very complete, but as they get more practice and listen to each other's reports, they will become better.

Keep your grade book in your hand as you walk around the room, making sure you can hear their oral presentations. But I also recommend that this to be peer graded. Once each student has given his or her report, the person presenting turns around. With the presenter's back to the class, the other students use a silent grading system by holding up one, two, three, or four fingers, with one finger indicating below average, two fingers good, three fingers very good, and four fingers excellent. Students enjoy being evaluated this way, and it helps them want to become really captivating speakers and presenters. Extra credit can be awarded to students when they can cross-reference their reports to any of the standards they are studying.

After all the presentations are done, break out the list of standards that need to be mastered, and let the students decide which standards were covered in the news items. You will all be very surprised at how many are identified! Then later the same events can be worked into other lessons, whenever they apply.

If some reports are not presented well, it is still important to commend those persons. Thank them, acknowledge their effort, and encourage them to compare their report to the others. This is a perfect example of not penalizing failure in order to promote success.

This is one of the easiest months of the year to establish the joy of successful outcomes. Every student in every grade level loves to write about the fantasy of Halloween, but they often have more skill at writing about things they really know about, so you may want to begin there. For example you might want to say "Write me a story about your car or your bicycle," and they go on and on with interesting details. "Write me a story about your room, describing it with all the details so that I can see it in my mind's eye because I am blind. Tell me where things are, how the windows look, and what is near the door." Setting the stage with an introduction like this is very motivating. It creates the want to write far more than simply asking them to tell you about their favorite shape and why it is their favorite. Once they realize that they are good at what they do, making up spooky Halloween stories becomes easier than ever.

Over the years I have found many books that lend themselves to being read out loud. One that I highly recommend is *A Day No Pigs Would Die*, by Robert Peck. This is an incredible story often racing with emotion. It captivates all readers or listeners, and we often stop in order to reflect on the feelings the book generates in everyone in the classroom. All students, regardless of age, enjoy being read to, and research shows that children become better readers if they are read to. You can use this book from probably the fourth grade through twelfth grade with minor adaptations to fit the grade level. Here is how I suggest it be carried out.

1. Let everyone know that this is a very special book with many life lessons that they will remember always. Everyone must be present for the first chapter. Once you read the first chapter, explain to the class

that this book is far too moving and important for any part of it to be read without everyone in attendance. Even though you would love to read a chapter a day, if for any reason there is someone absent you will put the read on hold until everyone is in school. This is a wonderful way to truly get the students to want to never ever miss a day!

2. Before beginning, pass out about twenty sheets of unlined paper, folded in half and formed into a little homemade booklet to each student. The class is asked not to put anything at all on the cover. It will be illustrated after the entire book has been read. The first two pages are character pages. As new characters are introduced, students should put their names on these pages with a brief description of who they are and what they are like.

3. You will read each chapter aloud. Once you have completed reading a chapter, ask students to summarize what they have just heard, including all the details they can remember, on one of the pages in their booklets.

4. Once you have finished reading the book, have students write an opinion paper and a character analysis. They may use any of the characters, not necessarily their favorite, just any character they can describe in detail. For extra credit they may also write a paper on the most touching or memorable part of the book.

5. Then and only then will they be allowed to illustrate the cover of their booklet. It will be judged on creativity and originality.

The learning that takes place in this lesson with the help of this book is beyond words.

As the leaves change colors, your students will have begun to develop new attitudes about work, school, and education. Autumn gives us all permission to leave behind what used to be and change into something new. Take October to imbue your class with the desire to do just that: grow, experience, and change.

At the end of October, give yourself another brief evaluation.

☐ Are your students taking notes, making flash cards, putting things in their portfolios, and coming in prepared?

☐ Are you keeping the Countdown going?

☐ Are you marking the days off the Calendar as they go by?

☐ Are you entering any new dates on your Calendar, such as when booklets or character papers are due?

☐ Are you and your students checking off the standards that they have mastered?

☐ Are you giving frequent four-question quizzes and putting the grades on the bell Curve? (This ought to be done daily if possible!)

☐ Are you keeping your class included in the overall goal?

☐ Are you on schedule?

☐ Are you making it clear to students that you are all on the same team?

# November

*A*merican poet, writer and editor Hendrick John Clarke tells us,

A good teacher, like a good entertainer, first must hold his audience's attention.

In November, we are so grateful and it shows. A gratifying way to get students' attention and entertain them this month is to make a Gum Tree! Cut out a large paper tree, and let them know each time they get a perfect score on a test they can put a glob of chewed gum on the trunk of the Gum Tree. Yes, it is childish, but they are children and love it. They truly think it is so cool and fun. Being silly along with them, setting reachable goals together, is very important. It sends a unifying message: We can have fun while working hard together in order to become winners together. What a wonderful way to model being on the same team.

Here is November, and you have the audience's attention as never before! The class is very involved. They eagerly arrive each day, and it is obvious they enjoy learning—and why not? You are terrific, upbeat, informative, and humorous; you click right along in a fast, easy-to-understand, and interesting manner each and every day. The students are part of it all, collecting notes, and rewriting the important facts on flash cards. And together everyone knows just where they are going, how long it will take to get there, and what it will take to get there. Attitude really is the paintbrush of life! It appears as if everyone's attitude is just wonderful and much learning is taking place.

You have a primary goal, an underlying mission at all times, to stay on schedule. You will no longer even think about teaching to the test. It has become so easy to look at a group of standards, then think to yourself: "OK, how can I explain these standards without a book? How can I explain these concepts in a relevant fashion?" You will have textbooks available to you, so look at them. Go through your textbooks and familiarize yourself with the information in them so that you are really teaching the subject, not just pointing students to a book. The textbook is now a tool they can dive into and immerse themselves in *after* you have thoroughly explained the standard and the concept. It becomes a review and therefore is much more understandable. Think about what needs to be taught, and use your own personal experience to put it into context. Then engage and empower students with a story that they can relate to that combines an interesting situation with that standards-based concept. This method will give you far more flexibility than just using a textbook because the class "gets it" so much faster. The class will remember the lessons with a deep-seated connection to you as well. They are often learning while not even aware that they are learning, and that tactic sets you apart from the average teacher.

Veterans Day is also in November. As I pointed out in the previous paragraph, everything can become a lesson. For example, every single month, with the exception of August, has a major holiday. Share this bit of trivia by again bringing attention to your Calendars and looking at all the holidays together. Veterans Day is a very important holiday and often overlooked. Sharing this can make them aware of places like the Military Academy at West Point, the

United States Naval Academy, the Air Force Academy, and the Coast Guard Academy, as well as important events like World War I, World War II, and the current wars in Iraq and Afghanistan.

Usually around Veteran's Day there are only about 120 school days left, and you should make sure to make note of it. "Over sixty days are gone. That is one-third of the school year gone, complete, finished, over, never to return again. Have we been as productive as possible?" Your August, September, October, and half of the November Calendars will be covered up with the standards your students have mastered, showing them just how much they have learned during the first third of this school year Countdown!

This is a great time to evaluate how well you are moving along by reviewing where you are in your Total Teacher Plan. Did you lay things out as well as they could have been laid out? If not, I hope you have lots of arrows and sticky notes so that next year can be even better. If we ask our class to be self-reflective from time to time, we must check our own growth and development as well. Students who are lagging behind (still on the far left end of the curve) can be encouraged to turn in minireports to share how other countries celebrate times of thanksgiving. Ask students to focus their current event reports on food, diet, and nutrition.

As another exercise in this food-conscious month, engage the class in drawing the food pyramid and providing a breakdown of what the phrase "serving size" really means. Students are often amazed when they learn that the human hand can be used as a measuring tool, helping people not to overeat. When we eat out, we can use this built-in tool, our hand, which is always with us.

- The adult fist is about the same as a cup.

- The adult thumb is about the same as one ounce of cheese or meat.

- If you cup your hands together, they can hold about two ounces of pretzels.

- Show them that the palm of the hand, without the fingers, is about the same size as a recommended serving of meat or fish or chicken. A serving of meat is also about equivalent in size to a deck of cards.

- The thumb is about a tablespoon.

- The tip of the finger is about a teaspoon.

They quickly begin equating these visualizations with what they actually consume.

Let students know that years ago a cup of coffee or a cup of tea or a cup of soup was truly just a cup: eight ounces and no more. Today eight ounces seem ridiculously small compared to the megaportions that we are all very familiar with. With this lesson you can almost see the aha light go on as they suddenly understand the reason for obesity being such a problem. A quarter-pounder, being one-fourth of a full pound (in addition to the roll, the cheese, and the dressings), suddenly seems like a huge amount of food, well over a serving size. At lunch from this point forward someone is almost always bound to make a comment about the size of something. Awareness is extremely beneficial, whereas lack of awareness is often what leads people to make bad choices.

In addition to the regular standards-based curriculum, during the week before Thanksgiving you can engage in creating a food journal. The class comes in each day suddenly very mindful of their food choices, with journal comments like:

"I need to eat more vegetables."

"I have not met the serving requirements in three days."

"I need to eat less sugars, or more meat."

Whatever the comment, the great thing is the amount of learning taking place in the best possible way, using real and meaningful application.

November and Thanksgiving allow us to reflect on our lives while keeping the standards front and center. Even though the class is wonderful, often there are concerns at home or elsewhere that make a child need more attention. This is an appropriate time to introduce the *problem box*. Share that you think they are all very special. Share also that we all have issues or concerns that from time to time trouble us. Let them know that we all have different ways of dealing with these problems. Let them know that they can write their concerns on a piece of paper, that they can remain anonymous, and that they can deposit the paper in the problem box. Tell them we will brainstorm possible solutions together during problem box time. The solutions are usually brilliant, and because they are their solutions, the class adheres to them. Sometimes students will blurt out, "That was my problem, what can I do if . . ." during the discussion because they want more feedback. Other times no one claims ownership, and it really does not matter. You will lead the group in discussions that will enable them to solve their own problems.

At times *you* may have a concern and may anonymously drop it into the problem box. "I really want to learn and listen to the teacher, but often people distract me because they are talking or passing notes. What can we do?" This may be a concern that you recognize and realize that to have a solution that they would buy into would be an enormous help to all concerned.

This is a great time to introduce a pros and cons list that may address these concerns. An enjoyable lesson that is often not taught in school consists of the different steps of problem-solving techniques or simply brainstorming any number of solutions, and then identifying a tactic that the class may choose to implement. If necessary, a peer mediation team can be formed, and the concerns can be handled by peer mediators who later learn to lead the class in beneficial discussions. Your heart will swell with pride as you see young students get really good at handling difficult situations, many times more impressively than their adult counterparts.

At the end of the month, it is time for another self-analysis. Take a look at your plan, and begin by asking yourself "Am I where I predicted I'd be?" Remember, if we don't know where we are going, we cannot get there.

☐ Are your students taking good notes during your class?

☐ Are you validating your students' efforts?

☐ Are flash cards being made and mastered and perhaps used by the students to quiz one another during downtimes?

☐ Are you complimenting dated notes, organized portfolios, and neat techniques that begin to improve?

☐ Are students putting samples of really good work in their portfolios?

☐ Are news events being discussed with interest, and are students' presentations improving?

☐ Are students who are lagging behind taking extra work home in order to keep up?

☐ Are you giving students lots of instant feedback in the form of quick quizzes and posting the grades on Curves?

☐ Are you being positive, not penalizing them for making mistakes, but instead encouraging them to learn from their mistakes?

☐ Is the class's vocabulary improving?

☐ Are your students aware of all of the standards that they have not only covered but mastered this month?

# December

*D*ecember and all of its holidays are all about children, and children are all about holidays. That is one of the reasons that the Calendars are so motivating. Looking forward to each upcoming holiday is intrinsically encouraging and can be incorporated into almost every standard that needs to be mastered. Let's talk about the things that matter this month, simply because the excitement that comes with this month's holidays creates a buzz that tends to overwhelm schoolwork. The smart thing to do is to accept that excitement and allow the class to engage in learning without realizing they are learning.

The first week of December warrants an intense review of the necessary pages that need to be covered in order to finish the current year right on schedule. Almost half the school year is over. That should mean you are halfway through your list of standards. Even though they are broken up in thirds, you can see that you are better than halfway through the entire list. An enviable goal has been achieved. It looks like there may even be enough time for a teacher-made midterm or two.

Your class is decorated for and even smells like the holidays. You've been to the dollar store and have all their little gifts wrapped and put away. They will be very excited when they return from lunch on the last school day of the month and find these little surprises on their desks. It is a fun month, and they are not thinking about much else at this point except the upcoming holiday break.

This is a great opportunity to teach lessons on marketing, common sense shopping, advertising gimmicks, and various holiday customs around the world. You will have the students' interest, and they will be learning without realizing it. Relate these matters to your specific grade-level standards.

The last two weeks of the semester are super special. It is all about giving and creating a special gift. It is about a present unlike any other, and your students will make it, take it home, and make the recipient happier than anything else ever could! The project is introduced this way:

Ladies and gentlemen, being a mom and a grandmother as well as a teacher and a counselor and lots of other things too, let me share with you something that I have learned over the years. Something that is probably one of the most important things in life! I'd like to talk about the joy of making memories. You, by the way, have given me so many wonderful memories this year that I can take with me no matter where I go, store them in my own private memory locker, and pull them out to be reviewed whenever I want to! Making memories is probably one of the most important things a person does! It is important because once you make a memory, it goes with you everywhere you go, never to be taken away. It is with you throughout your entire life, from beginning to end.

I'd like everyone to take out a piece of paper and a pencil. Now for the next thirty minutes I want you all to think of your earliest childhood memory, your earliest childhood recollection.

They will think and perhaps not be able to remember, then suddenly, *bingo*. They are all writing as if they were running out of time. They are recalling a special event that perhaps they have not thought about for a very long time.

Once they have written these earliest childhood recollections down, have them stop and explain the following.

> Ladies and gentlemen, it is a special holiday time, and I have had my classes make this gift for years. It will probably be the most cherished gift that is opened. It will make your mom or dad, or stepmom or stepdad, or anyone who cares for you proudly shed tears of joy! You are going to create a walk-down-memory-lane, a *Thank You for These Memories* booklet. This is how it will be done. Your caregivers love you very much. They are busy people, I'm sure. Sometimes things that mean a whole lot to people get forgotten, special things, and that is sad. Each of you has special memories that you can bring back to your loved ones. You will bring back memories of moments that they had forgotten, and it will make them so very happy. Perhaps they are not even aware of how special a memory this has become for you over time.

Inevitably a hand will shoot up, and someone will say something rather personal such as:

> "I remember catching a really big fish with dad when I was only three."

> "I remember my mom screaming when I put her red lipstick all over my face."

> "I remember my Grandma walking into the room. I was in my crib and she had a towel on her head. I don't know why I remember that, but I do."

Reinforce these recollections.

These are the very things I am talking about; they are your very own personal memories that matter only to you and your family. This book will begin with a letter. I will put a sample letter on the board, but you can make your letter say anything at all.

They are so eager to begin they can hardly sit still.

Happy Holidays [Mom and Dad, Grandma, etc.],

I am so lucky to be your son/daughter. You are the best parents [mom, aunt, etc.] in the world. I don't say it often, but I know how hard you work to give me all the things I need and want. You always come to my games, help me with my studies, and love me a lot. My present is not from a store. It's from my heart and my head.I am going to take you on a walk down memory lane. This is a thank-you for being you! I love you.

Once that is put on the board, they have a place to begin. They can alter it any way they want and personalize it to fit their individual families. One year I did this at the middle school level in my language arts class, and I had a student ask me whether he could make three copies. I told him of course he could, but asked why. He told me that his real father was in prison, and he wanted one for his Mom and grandmother and his real father.

I also explain that the booklet will have the format of a simple book. It will be divided into either birthdays or school grades. Organizing it like this makes it easy to remember when these memories took place as well as giving the booklet a chronological order. They start by taking notes on memories of kindergarten, then first grade, second grade, third grade, and so on. They begin with a rough draft, using the time line they created, then they rewrite and edit. Finally, they put all the pages together in a bound book, with each page being about a separate memory, complete with special words or poems telling the person or people involved how much they are loved. Students often ask whether they can include pictures. This becomes the project for the last two weeks before the holiday break. They love doing this and are on their own.

You guide them, helping with grammar and spelling, but it is their gift and they know just what they want to say and how they want it to look!

Math comes into play as students use rulers to center their writings on the pages or work out where to place pictures. Recall and critical thinking skillsare used when they chronologically organize and date their work. Artistic skills are used in decorating the booklets. The pride, love, and pleasure they experience in this project teaches them more than you can imagine. Often they ask whether they can do another for grandparents or a stepparent or some other special person. Everyone works at his or her own pace, and the sharing and pride you see now are repeated again on Christmas morning and once again when they return to school, telling you how happy the book made the recipient! They so learn the joy of giving! "My Mom must have shown that book to everyone in the neighborhood." "My Dad said that if the house ever burned down that would be the first thing he would grab!" There are usually only about ten school days in December, and often they are nonproductive. This project enables lots of learning to take place and time flies by! If you have access to a laminator, have them create the cover page first. Then as they are working on the other pages, you can laminate the covers. It's a piece of work parents cherish forever.

Of course, this month also lends itself to a grab bag, a name exchange, or whatever else you decide to make the start of the holiday break special. Let go of set schedules, and let this project whirl them into applying all they know. Your heart will burst with pride.

The students leave school, proud of the gift they have created. They even enjoy wrapping it in self-decorated paper, to really make it special and personalized. It is unlike any other gift they have ever created. Your students will go home and enjoy the holiday break more than ever because they have changed. Your students have become informed, aware, responsible, and, most of all, extremely compassionate. They are very proud of what they have learned about other cultures, and have a new-found appreciation for the different things that people believe.

You can give your students another gift that they can collect when they return. Tell them that you will give them 10 points for each and every standard that they know really well when they return after their time off. This is a wonderful way for them to begin the new semester with a strong accumulation of points that can be added to their grade point average, *if* they make the right choices while they are off. We have wonderful wise words from many people who have walked this walk prior to us. I think of Anna Quindlen, who tells us:

> If your success is not on your own terms, if it looks good to the world but does not feel good in your heart, it is not success at all.

This year certainly feels good in their hearts and in yours too. You have a really united team! Expectations have never been higher, and incredibly, everyone is rising to the occasion. You are now truly Totally Teaching. Have a very happy holiday with your students and for yourself. Give yourself a nice present for having introduced and taught two-thirds of the standards by this, the end of December.

# January

*H*appy New Year! The Total Teacher Plan has changed your life and the lives of your students, and many of the students in your class probably now want to become teachers! Imitation is the greatest form of flattery. You have been such an inspiration to them and for them. What a compliment to you!

During Winter break, you probably found yourself thinking of new ways to relate everything to something you are studying in the classroom. You realized things like that fractions and tonnage can be taught by comparing pickup trucks. A half-ton pickup truck is meant to carry one-half of a ton, which is half of 2,000 pounds, or 1,000 pounds. How much, then, would a three-quarter-ton pickup truck carry?

It was fun taking only your grade book home over winter break and writing out those brief thank-you notes to all the students for the lovely Christmas gifts you received. Modeling good manners is very important. The children who did not give you a gift should get a personalized note from you anyway, thanking them for something they have accomplished in class or just for being who they are and brightening your days. Whatever you share, they will treasure it forever. The point is that you can make every child in your room feel genuinely important.

The beginning of the new year is a great time to introduce the concept of writing down new goals, otherwise known as New Year's resolutions. Explain how they are working (and will continue to work) to meet standards-based goals all year. Now they can also make their own personal resolutions and goals and try to reach them by a specific date. Explain that the goals, or resolutions, must be attainable. Talking about setting goals is a way to engage the class in a practical skill as well as in a traditional exercise. They can write three specific goals, which should ensure that they meet at least one as long as they are realistic. One very attainable goal would be to learn and use four new vocabulary words every week from a list you provide. This would certainly guarantee a much higher result on their final exams. If students are weak in science or social studies, they can set challenging but achievable goals in these areas, such as map identification or learning scientific terms that often cause stress on tests. A great deal of self-esteem and confidence is earned by this very small but rewarding exercise of setting reachable goals.

Often when students return from the holiday break, they have lots to share with each other. I've found that students simply do not know how to whisper. Let me share a wonderful way to mesmerize a class and help them learn how to keep their voices down. Many years ago I walked into the library during my free period, and the Media Specialist was going out of her mind because the students were being noisy. I asked her whether I could interrupt for a minute, and of course, she told me to be her guest! So here's what I said to the class:

> Ladies and gentlemen, how would you like to learn a really neat trick that will keep you from getting the librarian or anyone else for that matter upset with you again for being too loud? [*All hands go up!*] OK, let me ask each of you to put your first two fingers on your Adams apple just like this. Do you all know where that is? [*I demonstrate.*] Now in your regular voice simply say,

"I am talking in my regular voice." [*They all say it in unison.*] Did you feel that little lump in your throat jiggle? [*They all shout a big loud yes.*] Now say it this way, "I am now really, really whispering." [*They all whisper.*] "I am really, really whispering." [*I then asked the pivotal question.*] Did any of you feel any jiggle?

Of course, they replied with a wide-eyed, surprised *no* and tried it again. I explained that we can't do something if we don't really know how to do it, and now that they knew how to whisper, they had no excuse not to do it. From then on I would laugh to myself as I watched them line up to go into the media center with their books in one hand and the first two fingers of the other hand on their throats.

We are now on the downhill side of the year, and everyone is helping each other. It's all about reaching a high class average by the end of the year. Learning the curriculum well so that it will be remembered easily next year, not just for end-of-year testing, is crucial. Making many of the lessons real to students is necessary. Check your plans and put them into high gear if need be. Don't allow the class to get bored. A great deal needs to be addressed in January. Lots of great ideas are blossoming.

Tape an episode of Kid's week on the television show *Jeopardy,* in order to introduce the class to some very brilliant children and give them a peek outside their immediate frame of reference. They often know many of the answers to the questions on this game show, which becomes very motivating.

Play a spontaneous game. Ask them whether they can think of any job that does not require math skills. Math is everywhere and used in everything. Something as simple as having to tell time in order to get to work on time is based on math. From a checkout clerk counting change, to a chef measuring ingredients, to a rock musician dividing up the band's pay, virtually all jobs involve math at some level. From the simplest to the most challenging of careers, *all* require a strong knowledge of math. They never thought of math this way before, so this really makes them want to learn more about math.

*Roll of Thunder, Hear My Cry* by Mildred Taylor is a wonderful book to read aloud for the month of January. Introducing Martin Luther King Jr. Day and why it is a national holiday, is better understood after reading this book. The book will capture the entire class as you read and discuss it. Have students create small handmade booklets for note taking on each chapter as well as a character page, just as they did for *A Day No Pigs Would Die*. Bring closure to the assignment with a character analysis and an opinion paper. These booklets can also be put into the students' portfolios once they are completed.

Another really helpful thing to do is to encourage the students to have a big box or a file cabinet at home where they can keep all their important work. Standards repeat throughout the grade levels, so this is a very useful suggestion.

The class needs to buckle down at this time of the year, and with the Calendars and Countdowns, this realization is suddenly their responsibility not just yours! Most of the material is now new, so some extra studying will have to take place in order for everyone to keep up. Make sure those flash cards and notebooks are dated and up to par. It is a new year, and the tone that you set will carry you through the next five months.

Perhaps a notebook quiz might be in order (or whatever it takes to make sure that everyone is working together). A note book quiz creates the desire to keep a valid organized notebook. Here are some sample questions:

- Question 1: "On Monday October 15, what did we discuss and deem important about Alaska?"

- Question 2: "What was the last item I had you write down in your notebook on Friday of last week?"

- Question 3: "What was the first extra credit assignment I gave you this quarter?"

- Question 4: "What was the date of our first entry in our notebooks?"

Students quickly learn that the more thorough their notes are, and the better organized they are, the better able they are to answer any questions on the material and the better the grades they will earn.

You may be pairing up students daily after their grades are plugged into the curves that show them where they are. This encourages everyone to continue with the mind-set of being a part of the team, comparing note books and helping each other with personal ideas. Each and every class has a different makeup, and you will figure that out quickly. Don't fight it, simply use it to everyone's advantage. Changing seats every week using the lottery pick keeps things fair. Engaging their awareness of how many days of school are left, as well as how many have been used up—never to be here again—encourages the validity of deadlines. The ongoing question at the end of each day is, "Were we productive?" and it is a very motivating question. We can't change what happened yesterday, but we certainly can learn from our choices today and make better choices tomorrow. There is an obvious shift. Much of what you always wanted to take place in previous years, now happens automatically.

When unpredictable current events are dramatic and problematic, allow students to think about solutions. Work with these situations to enhance critical thinking. The class enjoys this new pace a great deal; they work and develop commendable behavior and work ethics. They are no longer bored, a common complaint of years gone by. The days go by quickly. Much more material is being covered than ever, and it's all very interesting and upbeat as well as meaningful. This time of the year makes students very goal oriented, making their achieved New Year's resolutions very rewarding. They want to average their grades more often, and they really step up their own self-competition. Competing with oneself is powerful. Report cards go home in late January. It is a good month for everyone to do some self-reflection. Encourage students to make up quiz questions and spend some time each day quizzing each other. They particularly enjoy working in pairs.

Make time in January to compare a national newspaper, such as *USA Today*, to your local paper and perhaps to a state paper as well. This is a great lesson that brings home how much is in the world outside your community, state, and country. I always bring the newspaper class to a close with a story about an event that really bothered my own children when they were young. One day they were out riding their bikes and observed someone putting just enough money in a newspaper machine to obtain one paper but reaching in and taking out an entire handful of papers—stealing them! They watched the entire process and thought it was just plain wrong. They came home and told me, saying that when they grew up they would invent a machine that would prevent that sort of thing from happening. This usually gets me motivated to schedule an invention convention for the month of March: "OK, let's put it on the calendar for March, and if we complete all the things we are working on—all our goals met and mastered—we will take time out and do an invention convention." Talk about an incentive to learn, listen, and get with the current program! It really works—again something pleasant to look forward to. They want to do even more. The newspaper lessons are informative and also introduce to students who do not have opportunities to travel much the incredible amount of technology, information, advertising, and events that are covered in a national paper compared to the local gazette.

For Martin Luther King Jr. Day, you can try a very special project. Here's how I introduce it to my students.

Ladies and gentlemen, today I have something very different to share with you, but only if you decide you want to embark on an extremely grown-up assignment. In the past my students have aggressively and successfully chosen to get involved, but let me give you the choice. It is a project that I initially had to get special permission to introduce to my class and let me tell you why. Back in 1977, a very special miniseries, called *Roots*, was introduced on television. *Roots* was based on a book about slavery, about how we captured and brought countless slaves to this country. It takes you through a two-hundred-year time period. It shows how the Civil War began, how the Ku Klux Klan came into being, and how our country evolved from the terrible state of disarray that it was in. It helps students see that all races have both good and bad people.

I now have a deal that I would like to make you. You can choose whether you feel you want to get involved. Whatever we decide to do it has to be unanimous. Here is the deal.

We all must learn about the Civil War, about how our nation evolved, as well as learn how to write well ourselves. These are all things that must be learned before you can receive a high school diploma. If you think that you are able to comprehend a great deal about history and situations that you will need later on, then perhaps you would like to take on this project.

Now parts of this video are very gory; also in about two scenes in the very beginning, there are some women who are topless because this video is true to life and that is how women dressed in the 1700s in Africa. If you are too imma-ture to see this without snickering, then we may just not be able to view this. I am serious when I say I will not tolerate anyone laughing or acting silly while grown-up things like that are being shared. I will pause the video from time to time and give you knowledge that I have to help you through these parts of the video. If you can be the adults that I think you are, you will view this with sincerity and seriousness as you learn about the history of our nation.

Now this deal goes with an enormous amount of work. The final reward for you is that you will become incredibly good writers. It is a learning pro-cess that is almost transformational. I have witnessed students who used to hate to write, or just could not do it well, manage to earn an A-plus on their assignments. Let me explain how that happens. We view the videos of the series in forty-five-minute increments with another forty-five minutes being spent directly after the viewing to do two things.

First, during the viewing you are not just sitting back and watching. No way! You should be taking lots of notes. The reason is that once the forty-five-minute viewing is over, you will have to turn your notes into a written version of *exactly* what you saw. There is no creativity or rearrangement of when or how things took place. You are not searching your mind for ideas, or thinking about what you might want to write about, no opinions, no added details, just complete regurgitation of what you viewed, in your own words. I will put an outline on the board after each viewing. You will be able to use my outlines to help you write about each part of the miniseries. Once you have a rough draft, it goes home and you have someone read it and help you edit it, correcting your grammar and language.

At the halfway point in the miniseries, you will get your first opportunity to express your opinion and share what you think about the first half. Whether you liked or disliked what you have seen so far, you should explain why. Each opinion should be supported by three details.

At some point I will also have you write a character page. The character page will consist of descriptions of the characters who you think are important. You will separate them by generations. We will talk about that in more detail as we move along.

After your character pages are complete, you will also have to write a lengthy paper on one particular character, describing three character traits that your person of choice exhibited. You will use scenes from the miniseries that back up the character traits you chose to identify.

If someone is absent, we stop, we do not view the series if someone is not here.

Now, let me see a show of hands that will tell me who has someone at home who will be able to commit to doing this for you. If there is someone who does not have anyone to help them edit, see me after class and I will try to make arrangements for you. This is a massive undertaking, but each and every time the writing skills get automatically better. I once had a student who told me he used to hate to write, and now he wants to be a better writer. When he completed this project, it was eighty-five handwritten pages. When he had finally added everything he wanted, and turned it in, he earned a special award. The most rewarding aspect was when he said it made him love to write!

To make the project extra special, each page that is in its final stage can be put into a plastic sleeve and the whole project into its own three-ring binder because this is an important display of their writing and it needs to be protected. Have students cross-reference the dates in *Roots* with other events in history. Give handouts that students can add to their project: historical writings, time lines, period facts, and other things that will enhance this multigenerational project. Also construct a time line and do a family tree showing all of the generations that Alex Haley traced.

The students now shift from little or no homework to a great deal of homework, but this was their choice. This was a challenge, and they *wanted* to do the work that went along with the project. They made a labor-intensive choice that was self-motivating. They know that all things must be standards based, and they quickly begin recognizing many of the standards that they are now held accountable for, are present in this project. It takes about ten weeks from start to finish, so it can really be a major grade for the third marking period.

Remember to plug the various due dates of this project into your big wall Calendars to create the *want* to stay on a self-generated schedule. The class is then given the opportunity to accept or reject your deal. Once it is accepted, you confirm their deal because, although it is not really difficult, it *is* a huge undertaking. I usually give them an agreement (that looks something like the agreement in Figure 3.1) to sign and thereby to confirm their commitment.

Figure 3.1 Student commitment letter.

I _____ will commit to the *Roots* Writing Project. I fully understand that I must engage someone outside of school to help me edit my rough drafts. The projects must be done in a timely fashion. If I am absent and miss a viewing, I may be able to watch the segment during lunch, during PE, or after or before school and catch up on the necessary writings, but any absence must be approved. If I am absent, I will hold up the entire class, and that would not be kind, gentle, or responsible. I will check off the assignments as I complete them. I will turn in each final copy and earn a plastic sleeve that will indicate it has been completed. I will then enter it into the binder I will use throughout this project.

Student signature _____

Print student's name _____

Date _____

Teacher's signature _____

I go on to explain the details of the project.

The grading of this very important project is truly up to you. Illustrations can be used for extra credit. The grades may be used for different subjects if applicable.

Below is a sample rubric. It is important that they have a sheet such as this to work off of and to keep them organized. I often insist that the date of the viewing, as well as the due dates, be indicated on each sheet. The commitment letter, along with the dated sheets, stay in the binder at all times.

- Video 1 part one = 5 points, part two = 5 points
- Video 2 part one = 5 points, part two = 5 points
- Video 3 part one = 5 points, part two = 5 points
- Opinion paper = 10 Points
- Video 4 part one = 5 points, part two = 5 points
- Video 5 part one = 5 points, part two = 5 points
- Video 6 part one = 5 points, part two = 5 points
- Time line 1797 thru 1977 = 2.5 points
- Family tree, including all generations = 2.5 points
- Character page = 10 points
- Index with page numbers = 5 points
- Character analysis = 10 points

This equals 100 points; however, you can issue one extra credit point for each illustration as well as a final critique of the project in its totality for perhaps twenty points. They will also ask whether they can add other information, sometimes very applicable to social studies or history. I suggest making all you do be standards based. Remember, they all have a grade-level list of the state standards that they are responsible for, and giving them standards-based parameters will make them much more focused. You will almost have to stop them from doing too much. They will want to cross-reference the presidents in power at the time, news events, applicable inventions (cotton gin, etc.), and much more that they now put together as taking place simultaneously. This is the want to learn in full display!

Of course, it is your call as to how unified or individual you prefer this project to be. One of my students came to me and asked whether she could do an oral report. She wanted to be Kizzy (Kunta Kinte's daughter) and talk to the class in the first person. I said yes. Her rendition was so moving there was not a dry eye in the classroom. The interesting part about this situation was that this particular student was not very popular and she had several physical features that were often ridiculed by her less than compassionate classmates. Her desire to take on the personality of this character and give this oral report was beyond touching, as well as life changing for her and her classmates. Her peers gave her a standing ovation. She was so personally moved and inspired that she continued to make writing her favorite pastime! I got a letter from her years later, and she told me that our *Roots* project was a defining moment in her life.

Students will be able to find a great deal of information on the Internet about the works of Alex Haley and this remarkable novel. This project can't be praised enough. The special needs children in your class can do illustrations rather than the massive writing it entails. The class writes so much simply because they are given the opportunity to retell and to rewrite a gripping story that they've *not* ever seen before!

That is a very important part of this process. There is anticipation only of what is in the next viewing, and therefore the students are not rushing the writing process. They can only regurgitate the little snippets they view in sequential order, making their own writing flow, with a distinct beginning, middle, and end. The writing begins with minimal details, then as they *want* to capture each and every thing that matters, their details become lengthy, creative, and very well thought-out and expressed. Often parents tell me that helping them is so exciting because the children take on such ownership over their choice of words and how they want to capture and express every incident they viewed (and the parents did not see), making them the only one who can do this assignment.

*Yay!* Isn't that what every teacher truly wants to achieve—the students doing their own work and taking responsibility for it, with the parents simply supporting the students' endeavors? The students learn about dates automatically, and the most wonderful thing is that at the end of school, when you have so much to do, they ask whether they can review the miniseries in its totality without writing and taking notes, during the last week of school. They miss a lot of the "seeing" as they are taking notes ever so vigorously. When they make this request, I always say yes, because it is like an answer to prayer; they are so quiet rewatching this series and I can knock out so much of what we all know has to take place that last week of school, with far too much downtime for the students when the tests are over and the work is done (for them, but not us!). Many student bring back their *Roots* project binders along with some sticky notes and add things to their projects that they missed during the initial viewing. This is the creation of diligent, lifelong learners! What a way to teach and learn!

Let me wrap up this segment by saying that the importance of this—and of projects like this—are beyond measure. The students' writing skills are automatically improving with each account they write. It is amazing. You can see in the first segment that they restate in their own words, and blossom by the fourth and fifth writing! They are quoting, paraphrasing, reorganizing, and rewriting more than anything imaginable. You just cannot believe how much they write. Many choose to type their final copies, which is totally acceptable.

The earning of those clear laminated sleeves for their work is very important to them. There is such a statement of pride and closure as they carefully slide their work into these casings. The parent–teachers organization gladly pays for them once they see this project. All the students must get a three-ring binder, which helps them create a wonderful, well organized project. They create a table of contents, and they are always very impressed with themselves when they realize the number of pages they are accumulating. Their outlines become creative works and often color-coordinated with legends for various generations or characters.

Once they are pleased with their final written copy, the actual deliverance up to the teacher's desk is incredibly important. When they display that piece of work to you, they make a proud statement. Checking it off the syllabus and having you initial it and then earning that clear jacket is a process they look forward to (amazingly) over thirty times during the length of the project. Each time they add another very impressively preserved sheet to what they already have, they are able to watch their version of *Roots* grow and grow like no project they have ever done in the past. They are elated, and so are their parents.

This kind of success immediately makes you the golden person, and feeling like that sure beats having parents and principals upset with you. I'm sure you've had enough negative meetings as a teacher to last you a lifetime! With the Total Teaching Plan, everyone likes what they are feeling and seeing. We often stop and read aloud some of the interpretations the students are most proud of. This propels the students who were a bit lazy about getting started. After listening to a few really good summaries, those skimpy writers truly get inspired.

There are always those who need to hear how others do it before they begin. They then get the hang of it and try to write more—and they do. It is all about pride, comprehension, and lots of satisfying work, in addition to learning about people. The black-and-white issues in *Roots* are very well addressed, showing that there are good and bad people in all races. An enormous amount of learning takes place. I often pause at various places in the video and share prior knowledge I have to make them more aware of what is going on. I have never ever had a negative outcome. I've seen wonderful, motivation, a desire to learn more about life, about authors, about history, and about writing!

Before you show the video, it is really important that students know their states and state capitals, as well as some knowledge of our country and that particular historical period. A few chats about Harriet Tubman, the underground railroad, and other issues now all come into play for them, relating so much information and making it very meaningful. Again, once the standards are used to validate them, they retain those standards easily and effectively. I wouldn't recommend this project for below fifth-grade. Fifth-graders usually handle it very well, as do sixth-, seventh-, and eighth-graders. I also recommend other viewings that work very well, but you must make sure that your particular class has *not* seen the movie you are going to use prior to you showing it to them. I recommend *The Grapes of Wrath* or *The Hobbit*. I have chosen these over the years because they are my personal preference for the best ways (I think) to impact the students' attitudes in a positive way. I think that these two additional videos make them aware of how terribly hard the Depression was and the importance of a positive attitude in times of hardship, again driving home my favorite thought: "The problem is never the problem, it is the attitude about the problem."

This project is easier to accomplish in a self-contained classroom simply because of the flexibility, but I have seen it implemented beautifully in departmentalized settings with both forty-five and ninety minute class periods.

For your self-evaluation at the end of this month, here is a different spin, but one that will help you enormously. Have your students write an honest evaluation paper about the class. It might be titled, "Things I really enjoy about this class, and the things that could be better," or, perhaps a paper called, "I really need help in. . . ."

As you review the students' comments, remember that they are brutally honest when they feel safe. January is about new beginnings, and being a new type of Total Teacher certainly makes a great statement. It is going to be a great year!

# February

*F*ebruary is all about *love*, and this year your students really love coming to school! Everything seems to be clicking really nicely. Most of the Calendars you began the year with that are still displayed around your room, are now covered with standards that have been mastered. Remind your students frequently that, once a day is over, they do not get a do-over, so they must be productive and positive. The class has become really upbeat; they are, learning a great deal and love being told how smart they are and how much you enjoy them. Current events have made them far more aware of what takes place around them. Follow-up stories are coming in left and right. Students are comparing geography to news, places to people, and situations to the stories they have read about. It is so rewarding to watch it all fall into place. They have also really defined themselves as young adults. They now have specific goals, new future plans, inventive ideas, and a new sense of right and wrong as well as likes and dislikes. Parents are coming to you, thrilled with their child's visible responsibility.

This is a wonderful time to infuse even more of the adult world into their area of awareness. You begin to plant seeds, and they begin to do some research on their own. Try asking them stimulating questions such as, "Where do you see yourself in fifteen years?" or "What kind of a career would really excite you?" How do they envision themselves spending their days once they are adults and college is behind them? You will have to gently deflate the dreams of those students who think that they will simply become rich by playing basketball or becoming singers or actresses. Let them know that those things can be backup dreams but that they must think about the reality of qualifications for actual positions in the adult world.

By middle school, students will begin thinking and asking some very real questions about qualifications. You can present a great lesson by putting their career choices on the board and then helping them do research about universities and graduate schools that specialize in certain areas. They can send letters to the colleges or universities that interest them, or they can search on the Internet and request information electronically. If you have a really advanced student in your class, you can ask that the other students report their findings and contacts to that person, who can create a summary sheet for the entire class. This project, which has very practical value in the adult world, also supports many standards: letter writing formats, research techniques, technology, and more. The students get personally involved and love bringing in the mail that they receive from various schools.

Your class learns to major in minor things. Big things seem to take care of themselves; they learn to concentrate on details. They conquer procrastination and learn that it is really the thief of time. The class learns to discover, uncover, and recover all sorts of information that just did not seem to matter prior to this year. You, their parents, and they themselves are very much aware of how much they are growing up—how smart they are becoming each and every day.

True success is about goals, balance, attitudes, and, most of all, desire. Share the story of Helen Keller, who expressed this concept ever so eloquently:

> I was like an unconscious clod of earth. There was nothing in me except the instinct to eat and drink and sleep . . . then suddenly, I knew not how or where or when, my brain felt the impact of another mind, and I awoke to language, to knowledge, to love. . . . My teacher, Anne Mansfield Sullivan, had been with me nearly a month, and she had taught me the names of a number of objects. She put them into my hand, spelled their names on her fingers and helped me to form the letters, but I had not the faintest idea what I was doing. . . . One day she handed me a cup and formed the letters w-a-t-e-r. She says I looked puzzled and persisted in confusing the two words, spelling cup for water and water for cup. . . . In despair she led me out to the ivy-covered pump house and made me hold the cup under the spout while she pumped. With her other hand she spelled w-a-t-e-r emphatically. I stood still, my whole body's attention fixed on the motions of her fingers as the cool stream flowed over my hand. All at once there was a strange stir within me, a misty consciousness, a sense of something remembered. It was as if I had come back to life after being dead. I understood that what my teacher was doing with her fingers meant that the cold something that was rushing over my hand was water, and that it was possible for me to communicate with other people by using these hand signs. . . . That first revelation was worth all those years I had spent in the dark, soundless imprisonment. That word "water" dropping into my mind like the sun in a frozen winter world."

Students everywhere need to experience love and caring like that Anne Sullivan gave Helen Keller. Each and every person struggles with a personal handicap, and the caring, determination, and attitude of a teacher either elevates or defeats the student.

At this point in the year, there will always be a few children who still are not reading as quickly as they would like. Have them begin rereading the stories that you already read in class. They will have more success with stories they have already heard because the words will have become familiar. If they enjoy science, have them reread some science lessons. If a fictional story is a favorite, encourage them to reread that. Have a volunteer tutoring system. Make it rewarding for the student who is helping as well as for the student who is being helped. With every accomplishment the student with difficulty makes, give a point or two to the helping student, the one who is doing the tutoring. It will all work if everyone is doing his or her share. It is said that from those to whom much is given, much is expected, and the exchange will prove that. When you let the high achievers in on that belief, they will be happy to comply.

Look at yourself as well as the class. Step outside yourself and observe how you handle things.

- ☐ What if your mother was watching you do your job? Would she be proud?

- ☐ Be objective and evaluate all you are doing.

- ☐ Are things all moving along on time?

- ☐ Do some things you are doing need adjusting?

- ☐ Have you mastered being flexible while focused, and structured yet spontaneous?

- ☐ Are you able to recognize your own strengths and weaknesses and then make the necessary adjustments?

- ☐ Are you able to step things up a bit if need be and slow them down if that is what it takes?

Give yourself a huge Ta Da! You deserve it.

# March

*S*tudents enjoy looking forward to an upcoming holiday each and every month, and this month is no exception. They are also very much aware of how much they have learned, and are looking forward to doing well on the state exams. Their attitudes and thinking processes have been positively and productively transformed. They love learning about things they are interested in, as well as things that they now know will certainly help them in life. More and more each day, prior knowledge is tied together with somethig new in neat informative packages.

One technique to increase understanding of the standards students must learn is to read the standard and have students come up with questions about it. Here's a fourth-grade science standard as an example:

Magnets attract and repel each other and certain kinds of other materials. Apply electromagnetism to the real world.

And here are some of the questions students might come up with about this standard:

Question 1: "Why do magnets attract or repel each other?"

Question 2: "What is a magnet?"

Question 3: "What is electromagnetism?"

Question 4: "What might affect a magnet's strength?"

They then must provide three answers for each question, with only one being correct, creating their own version of a multiple-choice quiz. They frequently make the quizzes much harder than any that would be teacher or state created. Talk about enhancing comprehension of standards! Throughout all this, you will be accumulating a standards-based list of grade-level questions for the following year.

Different strategies and activities such as this will make March memorable because it confirms how capable you know they are. Another technique that's good for reminding students how much they really know is to allow them to each teach a fifteen-minute class. Each student will be responsible for conducting a lesson, including introducing the lesson, applying the lesson to reality, assessing the class, and grading the assessment. You create a pool of topics from which they can choose. As they work out how to teach each concept, they realize how difficult teaching is. Once everyone gets the opportunity to teach a class, they usually ask to do it again and again. What a wonderful desire to have—to want to teach others.

By the end of March there will only be about forty-five days of school left, and the standards will have all been taught. Have the students take a few moments to write thank-you notes to the cafeteria and janitorial staff. Discuss the many compliments that can be expressed and the awareness of what would happen if these people did not do *their* jobs! This becomes a wonderful validation of work ethic. The students quickly process that, if these jobs were not carried out and performed well, they would be personally affected.

Their ideas of nice things to say to and to do for these workers will melt your heart.

You are now on the final stretch. Those Calendars are no longer visible except for April and May. This year is literally flying by! It is now time to begin wrapping things up. You begin a really exciting Countdown that will indicate the small amount of time you have left before this school year is over.

Self-evaluation is now matter-of-fact. Simply ask yourself, "Am I still listening to understand, rather than listening to reply?" If the answer is yes, your classroom has truly been transformed to a student-centered, standards-based place of business.

# April

Can you believe it? It's April. At the end of the month there will be only twenty-one days of school left. It is truly amazing how these Calendars and Countdowns keep everything on your Total Teacher Plan moving right along. You have covered all the standards and are now beginning a review. What a statement you've made to your students this year, including:

- When people are organized and know where they are going and how they are going to get there, they have every reason to believe they will reach their destination.

- When people are aware and appreciative of what is around them, life becomes informative and fun.

Early in April a culminating pep talk must take place. I have delivered the message this way, but feel free to deliver your message any way that works for you and with the subject you are teaching.

Ladies and gentlemen, I know you reviewed a great deal during spring break. We made that commitment early on. Now, since we truly learned all the standards during the first three marking periods, we are going to review, during the month of April, *everything* that we have learned.

Dependent on when spring break takes place, you may be doing this late March or very early April. (In a year-round school, it will be about a month before finals that prep them for the upcoming grade.)

I have some very important things to outline for you, so please get comfortable and give me your undivided attention. First, let's look at our Calendar. Can you believe the school year is almost over? It has really been fun and certainly went by very quickly. You are great, superstudents. We now have fewer than thirty days before we must say farewell to one another. In about twenty days you will have the opportunity to make me and yourselves shine. In about twenty days you will take the [*name of test*]. All year we have had almost no homework, and we have covered everything on all three of the standards lists. You have mastered those standards. Let's look at the Calendars. Each time a standard was mastered, we put it on a sticky note or an index card, and we placed it on top of the appropriate month to *prove* that you, in fact, did learn it! *Wow!* Look at all those standards you have mastered. You also highlighted it on your own personal list. You collected all your important work every forty-five days, and we placed that work into your bags, which will now be returned to you. Here is all the work you did this year. This will help you study. Plus it is the verification of all those mastered standards that are up here.

It is my job to bring the enormous amount of material you learned front and center. You need to retrieve all of the things we learned and make it fresh and clear so that you can have the highest possible grade in your cumulative folder right after the state exam scores come back. All year you have seen that my work has been laid out with specific goals that we, together, accomplished. "Plan your work and work your plan" has been our motto. "Know where you are going, or you won't get there" was another slogan that we lived by all year. All of the endless quotes we have enjoyed and applied all year have helped us.

First, let me talk about the math review strategy. The three things that we will do in the math area to make the math scores really high are:

1. Take our standards and the math books that we have and go over four or five chapters each day. We will discuss the math ideas in those chapters and brainstorm examples that apply the standards to what we find in our textbooks. We will be cross-referencing our notes, our standards, and our books. This is why we labeled all of our notes.

2. Create word problems using our state standards.

3. Make a little study booklet out of the glossary in our textbook.

To use the book as a study guide, you can cover up the definition and example and test yourselves. I will spread this assignment out for you. Tonight you will be responsible for working with and learning the terms in the A B and C section of your glossary. You will create a little study booklet for *only* the A, B, and C terms. Do not do any more than that. I realize that copying the definition and the term and that drawing the examples will be lots of fun, especially as your study book begins to grow. I don't want you to go too far ahead. What I do want is for you to really digest and learn the A, B, and C terms really well. Tomorrow you will be responsible for the D, E, and F terms, and so on. I will map out the rest of our math review on the Calendar. We will also talk about how we can bring everything front and center for our other standards-based subjects. This glossary-based review is set up so that you will be getting some intense studying of all the math definitions prior to finals. The cover of your booklet will be illustrated after the work is complete, and it will be collected on the day after your math final.

These specific strategies work only because we're done. We've completed learning our list of standards, and this enables us to go through the entire list of what we are responsible for via the vocabulary that it takes to understand these standards. Don't be put out by the additional work. We made a deal on the first day of school. It was a choice about minimum homework until this point in the school year. You have been given all the perks and benefits throughout the year from me, and this is where you do your share of the workload. I explained to you way back in August that in April the rubber meets the road. April is the time of the year when you know all the standards, and now you don't need to struggle through the learning part but need to commit all your learning to memory. This month is hard; it will not be as pleasantly balanced as previous months, but that is the trade-off for having little or no homework all year long. You will really have to apply yourselves for the next twenty-five-plus days. Does anyone think that this is not worth the effort? . . .

I did not think so. I promise if you do this, there will incredibly high results.

Now let's address how we will ready ourselves for the other subjects. It took us one hundred and fifty days to get to this point, and let me add they were one hundred and fifty very well-spent days. We had the material introduced to us in comprehendible chunks, we discussed how the material was relevant to your world, and we then applied the material. Now here comes a question I want you to think about: What good is knowing all of this stuff if you can't retrieve it when you need it? It's like having this wonderful Web site and not being able to access it.

Now let's take out our vocabulary notebooks and our English language arts standards, as well as our flash cards and anything else we have that supports English language arts. Bring out anything that you have earmarked to help you study and share it now. I am also going to give you some time to get your thoughts and strategies together. Then I want to stop and hear how some of you are planning on studying, because I know you have some awesome ways to approach this.

Involving students in the planning helps them really want to comprehend all that they have learned, and they always do have some really good ideas.

We are asking a great deal of our students in today's world. We ask them to be aware, to play sports, to study, to learn, to relate to technology, to be respectful, to read, to practice, to comprehend, and to experience far more than we did as children. To bore them in the classroom or with our conversations or outdated teaching strategies is simply counterproductive. I speak to my classes as if they were adults. I never talk down to them or imply that they are less than they are capable of being. A great teacher usually has students that turn out to be even greater.

A great way for students to have tangible evidence of all that they have learned and are now planning to review, is to make a Tree of Knowledge. They will be working very hard and everyone likes to see their efforts displayed. That can be hard when you are studying, but easy to see if you clean a closet. That is why, once we clean a closet, we repeatedly go back, open the door, and look inside. It is a constant confirmation of a job well done! Of course, students will tell you that the Gum Tree was far more fun than the Tree of Knowledge, but this tree is going out in the hall. Crumble up some brown paper and glue it to poster paper so that it looks like a tree trunk with some branches. This visible declaration of what they know will remind them of what they know every time they walk down the hall and look at their contributions. Cut out patterns of leaves in different shapes, using several shades of green paper. Once a standard is restudied and there is solid mastery, the student writes it on a leaf, and it goes up on the tree. Students love to see everything they have learned proudly displayed in the hall on the Tree of Knowledge.

There is no stopping them now.

# May

Some teachers simply speak, others teachers explain, but Total Teachers genuinely inspire!

It is now the month of May, and all but one Calendar has been covered with proof of mastery. The desire to learn has been building for over thirty-five weeks. You have changed the music and danced a beautiful new dance all year with your students. It is now time for the crescendo. Everything has been leading up to this. It's a wonderful feeling. Everyone swells with pride and accomplishment. It has been a tremendous experience because you've had lots of company! The self-esteem has grown in leaps and bounds. Keep it there.

Of course, some of your students may have stage fright or pretest jitters; that is to be expected. Allow them to talk about how they feel. Make time for it. Ask them what is causing their stress; they will share their feelings with you because they trust you, so listen to their concerns. Use every tool you can to explain how prepared they are. Keep the pace going by putting a chart of the upcoming three weeks on one of the large sections of the board, right next to the Countdown, front and center. Everything that is coming up is placed on this very important chart. As each day is completed, erase that day from the board. This month the weekends are not for rest or play. They have had many free weekends and will have the entire summer off. So during this, the final stretch, students need to practice, practice, practice. Because their standards were divided in thirds, this is very simple. They take the first third of their standards and for the first three nights they review those areas with extreme diligence. Then they will spend the next three evenings looking and reviewing and studying the second third of their standards. And, finally, a few days before their finals, they will have three more evenings to look at, review, and study the final third of their standards. There will be a full day for open discussion about questions they still have prior to testing.

In addition to their obligations for reviewing the standards, all other things also get plugged into this large, very busy Calendar displayed at the front of the room, including things like:

- Awards assembly

- Field day

- Testing schedule

- Makeup test schedule

- Graduation

- Fines paid and book return due dates

- Orientation schedule

- Other school business matters

In addition to this Calendar on the board, on the first day of May each student will get a manila folder, and with rulers for straight lines they will make their own copy. Yes, *make* their own copy, do not run off blank calendars; making photocopies defeats the purpose. Creating their own gives them ownership over the calendar of events. I love the quote that this exercise always makes me think of:

> Be who you are and say what you feel because those who matter, don't mind, and those who mind, don't matter,

and the students really don't mind because they know it matters!

The students realize that they have several obligations of their own, and many of them plug in those in as well, such as dentist appointments, or a church or sports function. They sometimes have cafeteria debts, the need to turn in last-minute makeup work, and other personal things. Each morning the class—together—puts a big *X* through the day on their manila folder that has been completed. They know what they have to do, and they do it in an efficient, organized, and very timely manner. Figure 3.2 is an example of what this May calendar might look like.

I strongly suggest that students continue to review until the day of the finals. For example, you can give them a study sheet that outlines some really important skills or standards on a Friday, and then tell them that they will be reviewed and graded on Monday. You will be able to reuse your sheets from year to year, really diminishing your workload even more. In many cases the review could involve the parents, or students may choose to pair up and work together in teams. Word problems, formulas, and anything else that supports the standards for their grade level can be on this assignment sheet. You can add many things that keep these assignment sheets exciting: vocabulary words, state capitals, people they have learned about through current events, concepts, standards, and the like.

Here's one way to create these very useful assignment sheets/study packets. Throughout the year in the notes section of your Planner, keep a list of items accumulated right out of your lessons, your curriculum, your

Figure 3.2 A typical May Calendar.

| M | T | W | TH | F | S/S |
|---|---|---|---|---|---|
| | | **1** 1st 1/3 of Math Sc SS ELA *23 days left* | **2** 1st 1/3 Math Sc SS ELA *22 days left* | **3** 1st 1/3 Sc Math Ss ELA *21* days Discussion | **May 4/5** study 1st third of all state standards |
| **6** 2nd 1/3 Sc Math SS ELA *20* days left | **7** 2nd 1/3 Sc Math SS ELA *19* days left | **8** 2nd 1/3 Sc Math SS ELA *18* days left | **9** Open for group discussions *17* days left | **10** Use day reviewing test taking strategies 16 days left | **May 11/12** review 1st & 2nd third of all standards |
| **13** Final 3rd Math SS ELA Sc *15* days left | **14** Final 3rd Math SS ELA Sc *14* days left | **15** Final 3rd Math SS ELA Sc *13* days left | **16** Total Review many Q&A *12 days left* | **17** Testing next week *11 days left* | **May 18/19** **Rested and ready** |
| **20** MATH FINAL *10* days left | **21** SCIENCE FINAL *9* days left | **22** ELA FINAL *8* days left | **23** SOCIAL STUDIES FINAL *7* days left | **24** *UPPER GRADE GRADUATION* | **May 25/26** |
| *NO SCHOOL HOLIDAY MEMORIAL DAY* | **28** *5 days left* RETEST MAKEUP | **29** *4 days left* Clean Room Organize | **30** *3 days left* FIELD DAY | **1** *2 days left* TRIP TO THE BEACH! | **June 2/3** |
| **4** *1 day left,* CLASS PICNIC | **5** LAST DAY AWARDS, DISMISS | | | | |

standards, your discussions, and your text that you can use for a review. This enables you to easily gather items all yearlong. At the end of each week, just jot down math terms and problems, language art terms, situations that were special, and so on. If a date in social studies was important, jot it down right on the Planner. At the end of the year you can easily pull from this wonderful knowledge bank to make up four or five review packets. Then on Monday give them the answer sheets. Just run off a copy for each student, and let him or her correct the work. This is not about a bad grade, it is about responsibility. If you have involved parents, this is the time to have the class write a note asking for help. You have made students aware that learning is their responsibility. Now it is just about using extra help on weekends so that Saturday and Sunday are not wasted during this very important time. Testing outcomes will be forever placed in their cumulative folders. Remind them that their schooling is this aggressive for only about three weeks.

Many of the things getting posted on this large Calendar are not set in stone, and are subject to change. We must be flexible. Remember rigid bridges break. If they sway and bend, they withstand all weather and weight. If you expect change, it is not aggravating when things change. The class expects to sometimes erase their penciled-in commitments, and this will eliminate frustration in the event it happens. You, the conductor, must really work hard at orchestrating this final finish with grace and confidence—at all times with confidence. Remember, students take on the personalities of their teachers. Management style really matters in May.

Early this month get as much information from your school district's central office (and there is plenty) on state standards, test magic, practice tests, and any other preprinted review packets to help the students see the standards in even more ways than you have already exposed them to. Every district has tons of practice material, and there are also countless Web sites that the students will discover and gladly share.

It is really helpful if you provide students with a sample exam that they can work on independently for about two hours. This will give them a sense of the time in which they will probably have to apply themselves in order to complete a given exam. If your tests are longer, then let them learn how that amount of time feels. Also, give tests that use bubble sheets so that your students become comfortable using them. If they don't use them frequently, students are at a total disadvantage when they take their tests. If you add a bubble sheet to this two-hour study slot, they will be learning much about how it feels to work that long in total silence, having to apply total concentration, and figuring it all out without any help.

This two-hour study slot provides many other positive things. It allows students to work independently and think about the skills they need to have mastered and in place for these high-stakes exams that take place in under three weeks. It also frees you up to do many things. You have worked very hard all year, and this time lets you accomplish many pending organizational issues. The students should have the freedom of working on any test bank in any order. I suggest your packets are a mixture of all the subjects and standards because when they engage in discussing them—and they will want to vent—it will open things up so naturally.

During these review weeks solicit the input of the students who thought that a particular question on the study sheet was "easy" to help explain how they approached the problem. This brings explanations down to a very familiar level for the student who may be having difficulty. Work together. This is where everyone will engage in jotting down last-minute notes and listen to everything being said in order to learn all they can from each other. In this way, all the bases get covered. Fantastic brainstorming takes place because they have been diligent all year. But let's face it: It is a lot of material to remember all at once. That can be hard for the best test takers. Again, let me interject some logic. As much as students love Christmas because of the gift getting, they don't get all that excited about making Christmas presents in July. This is the same rationale. Give them what they want at the appropriate time, with certain stipulations. *You* are part of the picture. If *you* give them what *they want* for about one hundred and fifty days, they will more than give you what *you want* in the end. They have come to look at their class as one big victorious team, with a coach whom they want to please.

Early in the month, you should also review some helpful test-taking tips. Here are some specific to language arts tests, as an example:

1. Always read *all* the questions about a reading selection first. It will give you a heads-up as to what to look for in the reading.

2. Highlight only the most important words in the questions and the reading.

3. Be a detective. Find the answer in the reading. Remember, it may be worded in a tricky fashion.

4. Be aware of topic sentences. Use context clues, and don't be fooled. If there are two possible answers, there is always a better choice.

5. Don't use all of your time on a hard question; mark it on the answer sheet as well as in the booklet, and come back to it later.

6. Remember the Rule of Fives: On every fifth question double-check to see whether you are on the corresponding bubble.

7. Be very mindful of how much time you have, and be sure to leave some time to check your answers.

I am sure you have noticed how much more grown-up your students are now than they were in back in October; so tell them. The buses for the field trip have been booked since August; so remind them. Give them still another incentive to keep them in high gear. The more you compliment their effort, the harder they try. No one can make them put their running shoes on at this point. It's something they must do for themselves. However, they do take your lead graciously.

Talk often about destressing. Some students may express that they are nervous. Talk this out with them, explaining that it is a time to shine, not stress! These three weeks prior to testing will go by very quickly. How commendable that you have actually finished teaching all the standards and have had time to review and digest it all one more time for over a month. Not many teachers can say that; it really is all about being prepared. The mood is upbeat, proud, positive, and productive. The students are ready to prove themselves and eager for their opportunity to shine.

The last six or seven days of the year speak volumes. The students have looked at their placement on the class curve all year, watching it move little by little to the right-hand side. They have no doubt worked harder than they ever thought they could. They had more time to play sports, read, study, and interact with their friends and families. They became more responsible and organized. They developed an ongoing desire to be more educated. Once the standards have been completed, mastered, and reviewed, and once the Countdown has been reduced to a mere five or six days, students need a break.

Make the end of the year outing very special, all-inclusive, and outstanding. There were no other trips all year. Remember, the reason for this big late-in-the-year strategy was terribly successful and worked well. Your students kept their noses to the grindstone all year. It was their choice based on the offers you threw out at them, and the last trip was one of those decisions.

Of course, every class is different, so I will just list some of the ways that we utilize the last days of school.

- If you chose to do the *Roots* writing project, they will probably want to watch the entire series again and enjoy it. It was, of course, intriguing and informative initially, but they were very busy writing and taking notes while watching. Most of the students heard it all but did not actually see many of the parts because they were taking notes. They are very proud of this project, and reviewing the mini-series is a great way to spend at least three mornings. Allow them to bring snacks and drinks and pretend they are at the movies. You can do all of your grades and necessary paperwork during this time. This is a win/win week!

- Another memorable thing you can do is to have each child bring in a national newspaper and go through it, discussing what is going in the world right now, as the students prepare to leave this grade. This will make as much of an impression as the first day of kindergarten. Put the headlines on the board, and encourage them to make a mental note of the day's events. It complements how worldly they have become, and it brings closure to the current events they enjoyed all year.

- Take an afternoon to have students help clean up the classroom from top to bottom. Bring in paper towels and some glass cleaner, a case or two of juice and water, and some snacks, and make it fun. They will earn many a thank-you from the custodians, and the cleanup is a wonderful lesson in good old-fashioned physical teamwork. They will feel great about how they leave the room for the rising class and for you. A room really shines when thirty people clean every corner.

- Keeping last year's class average on the board during the month of May encourages competition, challenging the current class to beat last year's class average. Of course, they want to outshine the previous classes, they want to be the best, and each year it happens. Each of your classes will do a little better than the previous class. You get better, and so do they.

Your students will leave for the summer, but they will continuously return to your room. It's a special room. Invite them back; have them speak to your future classes about applications, flash cards, and study habits. Welcome them home over and over again. They will inevitably enter your room, take a deep breath, shake their heads, smile and say, "Things were so great in this room. I remember when...."

# HOW TO USE THE CD-ROM

## System Requirements

PC with Microsoft Windows 98SE or later

Mac with Mac OS version 8.6 or later

If you have any trouble opening the documents on the CD, try installing the included Adobe Reader and Open Office.

Note for Mac Users: When the CD icon appears on your desktop, double-click the icon to open the CD and double-click the Start icon.

## Using the CD With Windows

To view the items located on the CD, follow these steps:

1. Insert the CD into your computer's CD-ROM drive.

2. A window appears with the following options:

   Contents: Allows you to view the files included on the CD-ROM.

   Software: Allows you to install useful software from the CD-ROM.

   Links: Displays a hyperlinked page of websites.

   Author: Displays a page with information about the Author(s).

   Contact Us: Displays a page with information on contacting the publisher or author.

   Help: Displays a page with information on using the CD.

   Exit: Closes the interface window.

If you do not have autorun enabled, or if the autorun window does not appear, follow these steps to access the CD:

1. Click Start→Run.

2. In the dialog box that appears, type d:<\\>start.exe, where d is the letter of your CD-ROM drive. This brings up the autorun window described in the preceding set of steps.

3. Choose the desired option from the menu. (See Step 2 in the preceding list for a description of these options.)

## In Case of Trouble

If you experience difficulty using the CD-ROM, please follow these steps:

1. Make sure your hardware and systems configurations conform to the systems requirements noted under "System Requirements" above.

2. Review the installation procedure for your type of hardware and operating system.

It is possible to reinstall the software if necessary.

To speak with someone in Product Technical Support, call 800–762–2974 or 317–572–3994 M–F 8:30 a.m.–5:00 p.m. EST. You can also get support and contact Product Technical Support through our website at www.wiley.com/techsupport.

Before calling or writing, please have the following information available:

• Type of computer and operating system

• Any error messages displayed

• Complete description of the problem.

It is best if you are sitting at your computer when making the call.